ROBERT LOWELL

COLUMBIA INTRODUCTIONS TO

TWENTIETH-CENTURY

AMERICAN POETRY

JOHN UNTERECKER, GENERAL EDITOR

ROBERT LOWELL

AN INTRODUCTION
TO THE POETRY

Mark Rudman

COLUMBIA UNIVERSITY PRESS
NEW YORK
1983

Library of Congress Cataloging in Publication Data

Rudman, Mark.
  Robert Lowell, an introduction to the poetry.

  (Columbia introductions to twentieth-century
American poetry)
  Bibliography: p.
  Includes index.
  1. Lowell, Robert, 1917–1977—Criticism and inter-
pretation. I. Title. II. Series.
PS3523.089Z856 1983   811'.52   83-2092
ISBN 0-231-04672-3

Columbia University Press
New York   Guildford, Surrey

Clothbound editions of Columbia University Press books
are Smyth-sewn and printed on permanent and durable
acid-free paper.

COLUMBIA INTRODUCTIONS TO
TWENTIETH-CENTURY
AMERICAN POETRY

For Madelaine

Contents

JOHN UNTERECKER

Foreword

One can—I've just done it—read Robert Lowell's *Selected Poems* in an afternoon and a long evening.

Read that way, the poems cohere into a homogenious single work, the record of an "I" who emerges out of literature, history, and autobiography into the jumble of other lived lives and then, ironically, back into (reverse order) autobiography, history, and literature: an "I" who was Robert Lowell and who cloaked the fiction of himself, his family, and his contemporaries in the ingenious disguise of truth.

Reading a poet in this way is, of course, ruinous to the poetry. (No one can take that much of it in so few hours!) But for the critic looking back in a last-glance fashion, it does help to uncover those elements of a man's work that are "there all of the time" but that we fail to notice because we are reading too carefully.

In staring hard at an individual work, we can usually discover its major patterns of meaning and feeling: the dynamic of its statement and of our response. But nine times out of ten, largely because we read poetry, by habit and training, out of context (both small and large), we miss those different kinds of pattern that link poem to poem and book ultimately to book.

I suspect that the older he got, the more conscious Lowell became of precisely this problem. Certainly by the time he was at work on the third version of *Notebook* (1970), it was at the front of his mind. And, half-a-dozen years later, after *Notebook* #3 had evolved into *History* and *For Lizzie and Harriet* and new poems in the same form had emerged as *The Dolphin* (all 1973), and he was at work reordering this already reworked material for his first edition of *Selected Poems* (1976), he was clearly preoccupied with the matter.

"Much makeshift," he begins the headnote to the 1976 version of those *Selected Poems* and then goes on to explain what he means:

> From my last three books, I have chosen possible sequences, rather than atomizing favorite poems out of context. I have a few slight changes here, often simply going back to discarded versions. I have made no changes in anything earlier, except for cuts in three long poems: *The Mills of the Kavanaughs, Thanksgiving's Over*, and four of the five poems in *Near the Ocean*.

The words I want to stress, of course, are "possible sequences." But I want to give at least a nod to the notion that an atomized favorite out of context is—favorite or not of the author's or even reader's—a diminished work. Once we lose its context, we lose or distort some of its power. When it ceases to be part of the larger design—a part of a sequence, say, or a structural element in a book, or even something grander, a key ingredient in a set of interrelated books—it may remain interesting but its reason for being in the first place vanishes. (Try reading what is usually printed as Shakespeare's sonnet #65—"Since brass, nor stone, nor earth, nor boundless sea"—without preceding it with #64: "When I have seeen by Time's fell hand defaced." Or try reading Blake's *Songs of Innocence* and *Songs of Experience*, carefully leaving out either "The Lamb" or "The Tiger" *but not both!* Each one of these four poems can stand perfectly well out of context;

that's not the point. In context, both poem *and context* are enlarged and enriched. Some poems simply must have their original neighbors.)

Lowell's refusal to atomize a favorite by taking it out of context is so much at odds with the way most of us have been taught to read, the statement should come leaping off the page shouting at us, "Watch out for me! I'm the enemy! I'll blast your critical practices sixteen years past forever!"

For if we have been taught one thing and one only by the great bulk of twentieth-century criticism it is that a poem must ultimately be seen as an independent object. According to such a view, it is the job of the writer to turn out a heap of poems; it is the job of the literary critic to "explicate" selected poems, perhaps to judge in absolutist terms their degree of success or failure, and, under certain circumstances, to assign them and their author a place in literary history. I'm oversimplifying, but there's no question that the pattern is there and has been there for the major part of this century.

Such an attitude is, of course, anthologist in nature. And it is in the nature of the anthologist to abhor original context. But, alas, we are trapped into the anthologist's world. Who of us doesn't better remember, for example, the placement of Yeats's "Among School Children" among its neighbors in our favorite sophomore literature anthology than we do in its original context as the twentieth poem in the 1928 edition of *The Tower* (the "context" Yeats had very carefully fitted it into)?

However, it is not our habit of atomizing favorites I want to focus on. Instead, it's the "possible sequences" that Lowell is constructing in his *Selected Poems* and the slant of mind that lets him think in those terms.

Let me begin by framing a problem Lowell had by 1977 created for himself and his heirs, one that is, I think, unique in contemporary literature. It's this: by publishing—in total—a dozen different revisions, arrangements, and rearrangements of the *Notebook/History/For Lizzie and Harriet/The Dolphin* material (three versions of *Notebook*, the two full books he evolved from it, five "possible sequences" from the material in *Selected Poems* [1976] and the revised "possible sequences" from *For Lizzie and Harriet* and *The Dolphin* in *Selected Poems* [1977]), by so publicly reorganizing and revising published work, Lowell made a true *Complete Poems* virtually impossible. Unless *all* the versions of this material were to be presented in *all* the arrangements, no reader could really know what Lowell had accomplished. But no publisher would ever be likely to authorize so monumental a set of overlapping volumes. No, there simply will not be a true *Complete Poems of Robert Lowell*, at least not in any final arrangement that Lowell constructed.

What Lowell ends up with is a set of sets of poems: precisely the opposite from what W. B. Yeats, revising his poems and essays for a lifetime, attempted to construct: a perfected "final" *Works*.

Lowell's variants, each "finished," each "complete," gave Lowell no end of trouble, and he sometimes apologized to his readers not only for what he was putting them through but for what he was putting himself through as well.

In the third edition of *Notebook* (1970), he explained that about a hundred of the poems had been changed, "some noticeably," and that more than ninety new ones had been added. The additions, he went on to remark, had involved him in a redesign of the entire book: "They were scattered where they caught, intended to fulflesh my poem, not sprawl into chronicle. . . . I am sorry to ask anyone to buy this poem twice." (But notice that he sees the entire book as a single "poem"!)

He also knew that what he was doing would be likely to get him into critical hot water: "I am loath to display a litter of variants, and hold up a still target for the critic who knows that most second thoughts, when visible, are worse thoughts." But he was equally convinced that what he was doing was inescapable: "I couldn't stop writing, and have handled my published book as if it were manuscript."

Lowell must have been conscious that, unless he were careful, what he was doing could lead his books to share in the fate of many of the most important long poems of his time. William Carlos Williams "finished" the four books of *Paterson*, published them, then found himself compelled to write—as a separate volume—Book V, and died with bits of work-in-progress for Book VI still in his notebooks. Pound overshot his projected plan for *The Cantos* and ended with the work unstructured, fragments of incomplete cantos tacked on at the end. John Berryman, after *77 Dream Songs*, wrote hundreds more, published them separately as *His Toy, His Dream, His Rest*, issued a "complete" *Dream Songs*, then died with dozens of additional "new" dream songs still in manuscript.

Lowell, at least, did what he could to redesign things as he incorporated revisions and additions. *Notebook*—in all three versions—became a mine for *For Lizzie and Harriet*, all of the poems in the new volume selected from one version or another of *Notebook*, rearranged, and at least partially rewritten. (The finished product was, he felt, a totally new work.)

History was even more ambitious. Lowell took what he could from the three editions of *Notebook*, heavily revising some of the poems, rearranging almost all, and tucking in eighty newly written ones. He had been upset by the *Notebook* reviews and clearly felt that a new design was called for: "My old title, *Notebook*, was more accurate than I wished, i.e. the composition was jumbled. I hope this jumble or jungle is cleared—that I have cut the waste marble from the figure."

Though Lowell was certainly dissatisfied with the various

versions of *Notebook*, and though he couldn't stop the new poems from coming along (all of *The Dolphin*, written in the same un-rhymed-sonnet form, was totally new), he recognized—cer-tainly—by the time he established texts for his two versions of the *Selected Poems* that what he was engaged in was not some-thing that would or could be "completed" in any conventional sense—yet he also didn't want it to be "incomplete" or frag-mented. His solution was "possible sequences," something that he had, in fact, been constructing from the very beginning.

I am not trying here to be ingenious or to justify what Low-ell's harshest critics regarded as a hopeless muddle.

I think Lowell simply came to recognize that certain kinds of long poems can have flexible form: that there can be a pool of material, some of which can be organized as *For Lizzie and Harriet*, some of which can become *History*, some of which can be grouped as "Nineteen Thirties," and any of which can be reorganized, revised, and rewritten so long as author and/or reader stamina hold out—as in seven "possible sequences" drawn from this material for the two editions of the *Selected Poems*.

If the fourteen-line segments are seen as discrete lyrics that—with appropriate revision—can be arranged, mosaic fashion, into any of dozens of possible sequences, Lowell's late autobiograph-ical variants can be credited as a deft way of coping with the tattered-ending syndrome that has affected so many long poems of the twentieth century. His sequences can also, however, be seen as analogous with the process by which life is transformed into art: they represent not "a" meaning for life but variant per-spectives on a body of experience. The "meaning" is in each grouping unique and different. Whenever the components are shuffled about, new meanings, new perspectives, emerge.

As in rejecting the atomized favorite, Lowell here finds himself drawn into a position antithetical to another dominant critical notion of our time. If we believe anything, we believe that an author has to stand or fall in terms of a "final draft." Lowell is uncomfortable with the word "final." What he offers instead are a series of possible drafts. It isn't so much that a following version should replace an earlier one, but rather that it be seen as alternative to it—merely different. Like children, new versions are simply younger than old ones, not necessarily better. (There's no need to discard Johnny when Susie comes along; families survive; it's really possible to be fond of all of one's children even though one or another might be a favorite for a while!) Lowell in some of his rearrangements goes all the way back to discarded manuscript versions. What he ends up with is an assembly of sequences. What he believes is that poetry, which has as much to do with a notion of vital design as it has to do with "final" statement, can be, like day-to-day life, tentative, provisional, even improvisational.

If the structures Lowell evolves are improvisational in quality, the elements that one discovers on a whirlwind tour of the *Selected Poems* are anything but improvisational. I have in mind such matters as syntax and imagery, the echoing designs that let us say, "Oh, yes; that's Robert Lowell all right."

Some of them seem obvious enough.

From beginning to end, Lowell is in love with imperatives and imperative-like exclamatory first lines. Here are a random collection of openings. (Page references are cued to *Selected Poems*, 1977).

> Listen, the hay-bells tinkle . . . (p. 4)
> *September twenty-second*, Sir: today
> I answer. . . . (p. 29)
> We couldn't even keep the furnace lit! (p. 63)
> "I won't go with you. I want to stay with Grandpa!" (p. 66)
> My old flame, my wife! (p. 101)
> Another summer! Our Independence

Day Parade . . . (p. 145)
His faces crack . . . if mine could crack and breathe! (p. 169)
Half a year, then a year and a half, then
ten and a half—the pathos of a child's fractions . . . (p. 209)

A more obvious, though related, characteristic of Lowell's work is his habit of beginning poems *in medias res*. We are tumbled into a narrative—sink or swim—without any preliminaries. Here's a very random collection of typical first lines:

Her Irish maids could never spoon out mush
or orange-juice enough . . . (p. 12)
Meeting his mother makes him lose ten years,
Or is it twenty? . . . (p. 15)
We park and stare. . . . (p. 31)
What's filling up the mirror? O, it is not I . . . (p. 48)
Thanksgiving night: Third Avenue was dead . . . (p. 50)
The lobbed ball plops, then dribbles to the cup. . . . (p. 59)
Tamed by *Miltown*, we lie on Mother's bed . . . (p. 93)
Back and forth, back and forth
goes the tock, tock, tock . . . (p. 105)
The house is filled. . . . (p. 153)
In a minute, two inches of rain stream through my dry
garden stones . . . (p. 166)
We were at the faculty dining table,
Freudianizing gossip . . . (p. 197)
I tie a second necktie over the first . . . (p. 229)
A mongrel image for all summer, our scene at breakfast . . . (p. 241)

If there are persistent patterns of syntax, there are pervasive ones of imagery. Yet for years, I've failed to see them. Usually I have no trouble noticing obsessive imagery: Yeats's birds and trees, Blake's forges, Shelley's stars, Lowell's friend Elizabeth Bishop's shores and seas. Yet it wasn't until my high-speed tour of the *Selected Poems* that I realized how compulsively Lowell—

like Bishop—is a water poet. Titles should have given it away:
Near the Ocean, The Dolphin; but Lowell seems so internal a poet,
so concerned with the workings of his own mind, that I found
myself persistently thinking of him as in some essential way ur-
ban. And that notion has validity. His locales are frequently
houses—or, as Mark Rudman points out, cars; his settings are
often bedrooms and studies.

Yet what his thinking mind turns to, over and over, is storm,
river, shore, ocean. It's no accident, I suspect, that he chose to
begin the *Selected Poems* with a squall and to end it with a poem
dedicated to a Dolphin, a poem that culminates in an image of
his book as "an eelnet made by man for the eel fighting."

Between these poems, literally hundreds of water images
open out toward pond, lake, river, and sea. They are never neutral; almost always, they are darkened by the corrupting presence of man: "Here," in one of his earliest salvaged poems, "the
jack-hammer jabs into the ocean" and "All discussions/ End in
the mud-flat detritus of death" (p. 5). *Lord Weary's Castle* is awash
with such imagery; it floods the title poem of *The Mills of the
Kavanaughs* ("I think we row together, for the stern/ Jumps from
my weaker stroke, and down the cove/ Our house is floating . . ."; p. 38) and dominates the history of drowned "Mother
Marie Theresa." *Life Studies* is totally infiltrated by water, and it
is certainly no accident that *For the Union Dead* begins with a
poem titled "Water" and ends with a reference to the dismantled
Boston Aquarium. *Near the Ocean* is explicit in its imagery. The
group from *History* ends in ice. The group called "Nineteen
Thirties" ends in a poem that has as its central image "dew-
drops, trembling, shining, falling,/ the tears of day . . ." (p.
198). The group called "Mexico" ends, "The cliff drops; over it,
the water drops,/ and steams out the footprints that led us on."
For Lizzie and Harriet begins with an image of God as a sea-
slug and looks pointedly toward "The philosopher Thales who

thought all things water" (p. 209). Finally, the selections from
The Dolphin are totally water. "Fishnet," that begins the sequence, anticipates Lowell's own death, then evaluates his poetry in terms of a net that, like the dolphin itself, is designed "to
catch the flashing fish":

> Yet my heart rises, I know I've gladdened a lifetime
> knotting, undoing a fishnet of tarred rope;
> the net will hang on the wall when the fish are eaten,
> nailed like illegible bronze on the futureless future. (p. 227)

and—to quote it once more—*The Dolphin* ends with a title poem
that recapitulates his lifework as "an eelnet made by man for the
eel fighting."

In stressing Lowell's sense of provisional form and his more
comprehensive habits of syntax and imagery, I've done my best
to steer clear of the brilliant, flashing insight that characterizes
Mark Rudman's eloquent book. That stands by itself and needs
no support from me. The intelligence of Rudman's commentary
is a fit match for Lowell's own intelligence; the poet's sensitivity
that Rudman brings to a major poet's lifetime accomplishment
is sure, vivid, and—for readers unfamiliar with Lowell's poetic
accomplishment—immensely helpful.

Acknowledgments

After writing for a year I found that I had a few hundred pages toward a potentially endless book. At this point my wife Madelaine, who is a mathematician, began to bring her need for clarity and structure to bear on the project. No thanks are adequate for the endless hours she spent with me working on every aspect of it.

I want to thank Robert Hass, Jan Heller Levi, Phillis Levin, Paul Nemser, and Katha Pollitt for reading and commenting on portions of this manuscript; Ellen Frank and Richard Pevear for their scrutiny of an earlier version of the entire manuscript; Frank Bidart, Philip Booth, Elizabeth Hardwick, and Stanley Kunitz for generously sharing some of their thoughts and insights.

And I want to thank John Unterecker for his faith in me, for his labor and patience and his meticulous criticism of every draft of this book.

Chronology

1917   March 2: Robert Traill Spence Lowell, Jr., born in Boston, the only child of Commander Robert T.S. Lowell (U.S.N.) and Charlotte Winslow Lowell.

1924   The Lowell family moved to 91 Revere Street after stays in Washington, D.C., and Philadelphia.

1924–30   Brimmer School (Boston).

1930–35   Attended St. Mark's Boarding School in Southborough, Massachusetts, where he was nicknamed "Cal" from Caligula, and in his senior year studied with Richard Eberhart.

1935–37   Harvard University.

1937   Spent spring and summer with Allen Tate in Clarksville, Tennessee.

1937–40   Transferred to Kenyon College where he studied with John Crowe Ransom and met Peter Taylor and Randall Jarrell, who became his lifelong friends. Graduated summa cum laude in Classics.

1940   April 2: married Jean Stafford. Converted to Roman Catholicism.

1940–41   Taught English at Kenyon College. Studied with Cleanth Brooks and Robert Penn Warren at Louisiana State University.

1941–42   Editorial assistant at Sheed and Ward (New York City), publishers specializing in books on Catholicism.

1942   Fall: Lowell and Jean Stafford stayed with Allen Tate and Caroline Gordon at Tate's estate in Monteagle, Tennessee.

1943   Leaves Tate's to stand trial as a conscientious objector for refusing induction into the armed services. In October he is sentenced to a year and one day for violation of the Selective Service Act. Served five months in federal prison at Danbury, Connecticut and the West Street Jail before being paroled in Black Rock, Connecticut.

1944   *Land of Unlikeness* published by the Cummington Press (with an introduction by Tate) to generally favorable reviews. Jean Stafford's novel, *Boston Adventure*, appears.

1946   *Lord Weary's Castle* published by Harcourt, Brace. Widespread recognition culminating in the Pulitzer Prize for 1947.

1947   Won an American Academy–National Institute of Arts and Letters Grant and a Guggenheim Fellowship.

1947–48 Poetry consultant to the Library of Congress in Washington, D.C.

1948   Divorced Jean Stafford.

1948–49 Lived intermittently at Yaddo, the artists' colony in Saratoga Springs, New York.

1949   March: Lowell is institutionalized for a nervous breakdown. For the rest of his life Lowell would be subject to a manic-depressive condition, for which he would require yearly treatment as of 1954. Returned to New York. Member of a committee awarding the first Bollingen Prize to Ezra Pound for his *Pisan Cantos*. July 28: married Elizabeth Hardwick.

1950   *Poems 1938–49* published. Taught a poetry workshop at the University of Iowa. His father died.

1950–53 Lived and traveled in Europe.

1951   *The Mills of the Kavanaughs* is published by Harcourt Brace Jovanovich. Won the Harriet Monroe Poetry Award.

1953   Taught at the University of Iowa with colleague John Berryman. Students included W. D. Snodgrass.

1954   Began correspondence with William Carlos Williams, a major influence from this point on. February: mother died. Moved to Marlborough Street in Back Bay, Boston.

1955–60 Taught at Boston University. Among his students were Sylvia Plath, Anne Sexton, and George Starbuck.

1957   January 4: Harriet Winslow Lowell is born. March–April: West Coast speaking tour.

1959   *Life Studies* published by Farrar, Straus & Cudahy. Won the National Book Award for poetry and shared the Guiness Poetry Award with W. H. Auden and Edith Sitwell.

1960   Read "For the Union Dead" at the Boston Festival of the Arts on June 5 on the Boston Common.

1960–70   Lowell and Hardwick move to New York's Upper West Side where they reside for the next ten years.

1961   *Imitations* published by Farrar, Straus & Cudahy to a mixed reception. Won the Harriet Monroe Memorial Prize. *Phaedra* published. Shared the 1962 Bollingen Translation Prize.

1963–77   Received lifelong appointment to teach at Harvard. Won the Levinson Prize awarded by *Poetry* magazine.

1964   *For the Union Dead* and *The Old Glory* published by Farrar, Straus & Giroux. Two sections of the latter, "My Kinsman, Major Molineux" and "Benito Cereno" premiered at the American Place Theatre in New York. In 1965 *The Old Glory* won the Obie Award for the best new play. Ford Foundation grant for drama.

1965   Refused President Johnson's invitation to a White House "Festival of the Arts."

1966   Defeated for the Oxford Chair of Poetry by the English poet Edmund Blunden.

1967   *Near the Ocean* published by Farrar, Straus & Giroux. Participated in the anti-Vietnam War march on the Pentagon. Writer-in-residence at the Yale Drama School where *Prometheus Bound* premiered on May 9.

1968   The revised edition of *The Old Glory* is published by Farrar, Straus & Giroux, and the third part of the trilogy "Endecott and the Red Cross" premiered at the American Place Theater in New York on April 18. Campaigned for Eugene McCarthy in the Democratic primaries.

1969   *Notebook 1967–68* and *Prometheus Bound* published by Farrar, Straus & Giroux.

1970   *Notebook* published by Farrar, Straus & Giroux. On leave from Harvard. Visiting Fellow at All Souls College, Oxford.

1970–76   Residence in England.

1971   Robert Sheridan Lowell born to Lowell and Caroline Blackwood.

1972   October: divorced Elizabeth Hardwick and married Caroline Blackwood.

1973   *The Dolphin, History,* and *For Lizzie and Harriet* published by Farrar, Straus & Giroux. *The Dolphin* was awarded the Pulitzer Prize.

1974   *Robert Lowell's Poems: A Selection* (edited by Jonathan Raban) published by Faber & Faber. Received Copernicus Award for lifetime achievement in poetry.

1976   *Selected Poems* published by Farrar, Straus & Giroux.

1977   *Day by Day* published by Farrar, Straus & Giroux. Won National Book Critics Circle Award. *Selected Poems,* revised edition, published by Farrar, Straus & Giroux. Received American Academy and Institute of Arts and Letters National Medal for Literature. Returned to the United States and spent the summer in Castine, Maine, with Elizabeth Hardwick. September 12: died in New York City. September 16: funeral in Boston. Burial in family plot at Dunbarton, New Hampshire.

1978   Lowell's translation of the *Oresteia of Aeschylus* is posthumously published by Farrar, Straus & Giroux.

Abbreviations

In the text the following abbreviations will be used for works and commentary by Lowell:

SP   *Robert Lowell: Selected Poems*, Revised Edition (New York: Farrar, Straus & Giroux, 1977).

LS   *Life Studies* (New York: Farrar, Straus & Cudahy, 1959).

I   *Imitations* (New York: Farrar, Straus & Cudahy, 1961).

N   *Notebook* (New York: Farrar, Straus & Giroux, 1970).

OG   *The Old Glory* (New York: Farrar, Straus & Giroux, 1965).

DBD   *Day by Day* (New York: Farrar, Straus & Giroux, 1977).

PRI   Frederick Seidel, "An Interview With Robert Lowell," *Writers at Work: The* PARIS REVIEW *Interviews*, Second Series (New York: Viking, 1963).

LCR   Transcriptions from *Robert Lowell Reading His Own Poems, October 31, 1960* (Library of Congress Recording), selected by Stanley Kunitz.

OA   *The Oresteia of Aeschylus*, trans. by Lowell (New York: Farrar, Straus & Giroux, 1978).

Introduction

> For where one finds commensurability with
> paraphrase, there the sheets have not been
> rumpled; there poetry has not, so to speak,
> spent the night.
> —Osip Mandelstam,
> "Conversation About Dante"

The relationship between childhood and landscape and language and imagination are integral to the poetry of Robert Lowell and account for the deep hold it has on us. "The Quaker Graveyard in Nantucket" and "For the Union Dead" are two of Lowell's most likely to be remembered poems. And both are rooted in prior experiences of a place, or landscape: experiences in childhood that prompt a profound receptivity later on when the boy becomes a man. In these two poems, still laden with the child's vulnerability, the poet parries some powerful blows, faces something worse than the worst he could think of—external events that exceed his own inherent morbidity: the death of his cousin Warren Winslow by torpedo blast, in the first; the neglect of the Aquarium and the destruction of the Boston Common by "yellow dinosaur steamshovels," in the second. Only then, after these confrontations, can his tone soften and sadness weave itself around the imagined scene.

꙲

I was on the beach at Madaket the day Lowell died. Passing Winslow Point on a bicycle in a heavy drizzle I remembered "The Quaker Graveyard" (*SP* 6–10) and how electrified I was when I first read the line "A brackish reach of shoal off Madaket." The Nantucket landscape reminded me of the language-thrust in the poem. There was the sea, impinging on all sides, walled out by dunes and cliffs, natural fortresses. And there was the harsh beach grass, and the wind flailing my eyes. I was struck—literally blinded—by the tenuousness of existence in a place where the elements vent themselves fiercely—"The winds' wings beat upon the stones, . . . and scream." It would take as much luck as skill to even light a match in such a wind and human dwellings look so fragile. There is aggression in the wind on Nantucket; how often the windows must rattle and howl!

I searched for a hollow to stay out of the wind and keep the sand from being blown in my face, spread the poncho in a cleft pocket of sand between two thin clumps of rough, spiky dune grass, got out my copy of *The Big Sleep* and suddenly remembered that I had once by accident sat next to Lowell and his daughter during a double feature of *The Treasure of the Sierra Madre* and *The Big Sleep* at the New Yorker Theater. That was in 1970. I kept trying not to look and see if it were really Lowell, and managed to keep my eyes trained on the screen.

I was in the middle of *The Big Sleep* where Marlowe has solved the case as far as his employers the Sternwoods are concerned, but he feels invaded by his own emptiness and decides—in a gesture that is decisive for the future of the detective genre—to bust the case wide open because he has nothing better to do; he's interested in smoking out all the corruption the Sternwoods want to keep covered up. Marlowe acts out of boredom, the full horror vacui of Baudelairian ennui, not out of malice or for that matter a sense of justice.

> It's BOREDOM. Tears have glued its eyes together.
> You know it well, my Reader. This obscene
> beast chain-smokes yawning for the guillotine—
> you—hypocrite Reader—my double—my brother!
> ("To the Reader," *I* 47; Baudelaire: *Au lecteur*)

A connection forces its way into my mind between the art of detection and the art of poetry. Lowell is adept at collecting evidence.

> A single man stands like a bird-watcher,
> and scuffles the pepper and salt snow
> from a discarded, gray
> Westinghouse Electric cable drum.
> He cannot discover America by counting
> the chains of condemned freight-trains
> from thirty states. They jolt and jar
> and junk in the siding below him.
> ("The Mouth of the Hudson," *SP* 104)

The search for clues, the way he chooses his details, and his ability to preserve differences between individual people, landscapes, and objects with such specificity have something in common with the detective's method of solving the case.

> He has trouble with his balance.
> His eyes drop,
> and he drifts with the wild ice
> ticking seaward down the Hudson,
> like the blank sides of a jig-saw puzzle.
> ("The Mouth of the Hudson," *SP* 104)

The Big Sleep has no solution. Lowell's life has no solution. His guilt, which is his persistent theme, is unexpungable, sourceless; I can find no bottom to it. It all comes down to, what you might call, desire. As Lacan says,

> There is no other way of conceiving the indestructibility of un-
> conscious desire—in the absence of a need which, when forbid-
> den satisfaction, does not sicken and die, even if it means the
> destruction of the organism itself. It is in a memory . . . that is
> found the chain that *insists* on reproducing itself in the transfer-
> ence, and which is the chain of dead desire.[1]

❦

The success of Lowell's poems often depends on his ability
to render believable characters, *others*, and so he gives us a riot
of particulars from which we must reconstruct them, giving the
illusion, through the litany of proper nouns, especially names,
that the world in his poems is tangibly there. More outwardly
weird poets are not as genuinely strange as Lowell.

> In the grandiloquent lettering on Mother's coffin,
> *Lowell* had been misspelled *LOVEL.*
> The corpse
> was wrapped like *panettone* in Italian tinfoil.
>   ("Sailing Home from Rapallo," *SP* 84)

I wonder what a non-English-speaking reader would make of
these lines, especially as memories of the details recede. (Robert
Frost said that poetry was what was lost in translation.) Forgetting that Lowell was a *Lowell*, I think the wonderful/horrible
play on *love* and *shovel* will remain interesting and comprehensible, and the reductio ad absurdum of the start of the afterlife in
all that mummifying winding-sheet will still signify that the one
thing worse than lowliness is expectations that are locked in a
time warp.

So much for the sense. I like the stately cadence, the way

he slows you down and holds you back at the start, forcing you to pronounce every syllable, to witness death at work, which makes you reflect on words, language, how they *work*, and the way he makes you read the part of the penultimate line that isn't there, the white space after the *corpse* stretching to infinity like a blank canvas, because the rest of the line is unutterable and must be passed over in silence.

✣

There is no way for any memory to be conjured up: it exists on the horizon line between sleep and waking—in the brain. Sleep brings it up. The body remembers what it wants to remember. Every poem is a facet of death. The best poems are bridges between ecstasy and death, the inseparables that can't be dealt with at the same time to any conclusion.

R. P. Blackmur wrote: "Style is the quality of the act of perception." In poetry this comes through in the freshness, the flush, of the language, knocking about among the things it has engendered, energy moving through a field of neutral objects, gathering and binding them by affinity or the lack of it. The poem begins in the voice, in rhythm; seeing can only be the start of it: the poem, being a verbal object, begins in the act of some bodily agitation, undetected, at first, by consciousness. I mean by all this to say we have to talk about style from the inside out, from the perceiving mind to the thing perceived.

Be it elegy or song, a poem ought to pierce the crisis of the imagination's instant, in which everything is always being revealed, uncovered, rescued from repression. Imagination demands a temporary death of the worldly ego, the censor, super-ego, commentator; call it what you will, it can't be contrived, only invited, beckoned (that is an individual matter); but there

are laws in imagination, taken as a distinct entity, that can't be
expunged.

In Lowell's best work the world in his poems is held under
a steady, unrelenting focus: there is the fact of something regis-
tered and held there, never the mental play that surrounds and
alters and shades the fact. It is a matter, finally, of dialectic: the
mind needs to be opposed, set against the fact of things. The
quality of the language has to be connected to some prior violence of thought, the outgrowth of a given pressure.

> O to break loose, like the chinook
> salmon jumping and falling back,
> nosing up to the impossible
> stone and bone-crushing waterfall—
> raw-jawed, weak-fleshed there, stopped by ten
> steps of the roaring ladder, and then
> to clear the top on the last try,
> alive enough to spawn and die.
>
> ("Waking Early Sunday Morning," *SP* 141)

There is violence in the poems but it is not conjured up for
its own sake. It is as piercing and clear and desperate and pathetic as the cry of the swan in his *imitation* of Baudelaire's *Le
Cygne*. Exile is a palliative compared to this:

> I saw a swan that had escaped its cage,
> and struck its dry wings on the cobbled street,
> and drenched the curbing with its fluffy plumage.
> Beside a gritty gutter, it dabbed its feet,
>
> and gobbled at the dust to stop its thirst.
> Its heart was full of its blue lakes, and screamed:
> "Water, when will you fall? When will you burst,
> oh thunderclouds?" How often I have dreamed

> I see this bird like Ovid exiled here
> in Paris, its Black Sea—it spears and prods
> its snake-head at our blue, ironic air,
> as if it wanted to reproach the gods.
>
> ("The Swan," *I* 57–58; Baudelaire: *Le cygne*)

Lowell is sensory without being sensuous. In this imitation he makes a beautiful and characteristic projection. "Le coeur plein de son beau lac natal,"[2] becomes "Its heart was full of its blue lakes," which turns "beau lac natal" into a fused image, "blue lakes," rather than a sacred space, "beautiful native lake." Baudelaire could transform his room into a resplendent den, open enchanted corridors in any niche, infuse neutral objects with an aura; he cultivated "art to enhance." He made the ugly beautiful. Lowell loves the ugly, the more lowly-than-he things of this world:

> Vermin run for their unstopped holes;
> in some dark nook a fieldmouse rolls
> a marble, hours on end, then stops;
> the termite in the woodwork sleeps—
>
> ("Waking Early Sunday Morning," *SP* 141)

And his bird would be the exiled swan's doppelganger: "Crows maunder on the petrified fairway" ("Waking in the Blue," *SP* 87).

Exile sets up a breach between the self and the world, a gap for the poem to fill. We feel this gap unabashedly as children, and poetry needs the awed bewilderment of childhood to get on its way. Translating from another language is one way to re-create this feeling of estrangement. But often when Lowell had a chance to do more than use the subject of spiritual exile as a literary theme, he repressed it completely and robbed his version of any tenderness. Compare:

> Aussi devant ce Louvre une image m'opprime:
> Je pense à mon grand cygne, avec ses gestes fous,

> Comme les exilés, ridicule et sublime,
> Et rongé d'un désir sans trêve! . . .[3]

with:

> Here by the Louvre my symbol oppresses me:
> I think of the great swan hurled from the blue,
> heroic, silly—like a refugee
> dogged by its griping angst—
>
> ("The Swan," *I* 58; Baudelaire: *Le cygne*)

❦

In his *Notes*, the painter André Derain speaks of the "difficulty in writing down one's secret thoughts in the practice of an art." This is the difficulty that Lowell is willing to encounter head on, the taboo he broaches. He maintains no illusions and sees death everywhere, in everything. Bark withers under his gaze. His poems smell of mortality, and this is why they can cause revulsion in the reader: there is nothing to set them off, give relief. There is no counterpoint to the dread, other than a kind of black humor. "All discussions// End in the mud-flat detritus of death" ("Colloquy in Black Rock," *SP* 5). The ganglia of his imagination are drawn toward the raw underside of things: the undertides. The tension makes itself evident in the gravid music of his verse, in the controlled explosiveness.

> Now Paris, our black classic, breaking up
> like killer kings on an Etruscan cup.
>
> ("Beyond the Alps," *SP* 56)

Lowell is a master of the fused image, moments of inscrutable metonymy, of half clear, *clair-obscure*, absolutes. And the words could not be so powerful if there weren't firm substance, terra firma, world, standing behind them, underneath them: the magic of Lowell's best work lies in how he conveys resonant sensations, evokes the invisible underneath the empirical frame of his poems.

When a society is intent on destroying itself, how can an individual keep his sanity, and to what end, and in what context? In *The Bow and the Lyre* Octavio Paz says: "There is no self, and within each one of us diverse voices are in conflict." But there is a self, and the presence of those diverse voices in conflict is its condition; the self constitutes itself out of them.

So much of Lowell's work had to do with coming to terms, taking stock, reckoning, as though he felt it was his duty to write autobiographically in order to give an account of himself. But who was the addressee? Or who were they? His wives and lovers and friends, a plethora of others, or were they stand-ins for himself as another yet-to-be discovered self? Lowell was his own patron; how could he better serve this patron than to do self-portraits, or, when he portrayed people out of history, to make them as much like himself, his patron, as possible?

In Lowell's work the data, the dazzle of details about his life stand for the more mysterious—less fixed—inner world. Words were calmatives for Lowell. And he could defuse his terror, his feeling of being ajar in the presence of other people by naming the objects of his dread: and in poetry objects and people, the inanimate and the animate, are similarly fixed, pinned down.

> I watch a glass of water wet
> with a fine fuzz of icy sweat,
> silvery colors touched with sky,
> serene in their neutrality—
> yet if I shift, or change my mood,
> I see some object made of wood,
> background behind it of brown grain,
> to darken it, but not to stain.
>
> ("Waking Early Sunday Morning," *SP* 142)

❦

There's hardly any poetry that has so many signifiers, so many details, so much data, as Lowell's. The precision of observed detail makes a poem timebound, contingent and, because it's a single moment of time, unrepeatable. Lowell looks at things in their raw particularity just long enough to make you shudder. He lets each image develop just slowly enough to get right under your skin, stick, stay there, and then it's gone. The image is gone, the feeling remains.

Those who long for poetry to be true in the factual sense will find no comfort in such poems as this one in *Life Studies.*

> Your stuffed duck craned toward Harvard from my trunk:
> its bill was a black whistle, and its brow
> was high and thinner than a baby's thumb;
> its webs were tough as toenails on its bough.
> It was your first kill; you had rushed it home,
> pickled in a tin wastebasket of rum—
> it looked through us, as if it'd died dead drunk.
> You must have propped its eyelids with a nail,
> and yet it lived with us and met our stare,
> Rabelaisian, lubricious, drugged. . . .
>
> ("To Delmore Schwartz," *SP* 63)

The duck here, no matter how vividly rendered, is emblematic of Lowell's relationship to imagination and his friendship with Delmore. "The stuffed duck wasn't Delmore's—'I've never shot anything but pool,' he told Lowell."[4]

The key to Lowell's poetry is that, like any good poet or artist, he always submits the facts to the transforming power of the imagination and the necessity it dictates.

❦

The dusty leaves and frizzled lilacs gear
This garden of the elders with baroque
And prodigal embellishments . . .
>   ("At the Indian Killer's Grave," *SP* 24)

The heron warps its neck, a broken pick,
To study its reflection on the scales,
Or knife-bright shards of water lilies, quick
In the dead autumn water with their snails
And water lice. . . .
>   ("The Mills of the Kavanaughs," *SP* 37)

Reading passages of acute observation, such as these, has made me think about what it means to pay very close, as microscopic as possible, attention to detail, to perceive with effort, as Van Gogh or Cézanne perceived, working day by day to fix the objects of their consciousness, rather than receive, as Miró received, visions of a timeless imagined realm. As now, I keep glancing at the calendar on my watch wondering why it is so cold if it is nearly May. Most of the ailanthus in Washington Square Park are bare, but a few, less recently implanted, hang in wispy clusters. There is the usual babel of noise from the massed transistor cassette AM blast radios. The chill air and flat transparent distances make things stand out in relief: the shadows of some branches on a red wall verge on the articulate; forsythia is blinding. On a lake in Central Park the rattle of oarlocks and splash of paddles and laughter; willows, pale green, luxurious; some kids scuttling hide and go seek up the rock on which the island rests; a dead fish; no tide. What we are taught to think of as the trimmings in any art are actually the fretwork of survival. Death is the connective tissue.

Not all poets work at seeing. It isn't necessary to be descriptive in a poem, or delineate the represented objects. Cars can be cars, they don't have to be Mustangs or Thunderbirds. But they do for Lowell.

> Father had had two coronaries.
> He still treasured underhand economies,
> but his best friend was his little black Chevy,
> garaged like a sacrificial steer
> with gilded hooves,
> yet sensationally sober,
> and with less side than an old dancing pump.
>
> ("Terminal Days at Beverly Farms," *SP* 79)

What fascinates me is how well Lowell could weave his words out of the fibers of the world. He was one of the few American poets of his time who responded to Rimbaud's injunction that the poet must become a *seer*, and to accomplish this must practice the systematic derangement of the senses. And even as his energy waned, and his imagination withered, Lowell would still confront the world that was given to him head on. "Risk was his métier" ("Ulysses and Circe," *DBD* 8). Francis Ponge, writing on Picasso, said in regard to his ability to enact continual transformations, "To err is divine." Lowell had the ability to salvage the most intractable material, like an archaeologist. He saw more deeply than he knew, and could, given the chance, find significance, fuel for revelation, in the most poetically unpromising place. And he howled with the horror of a wounded beast in captivity.

> Behind me! You! Again I feel the light
> lighten my leaded eyelids, while the gray
> skulled horses whinny for the soot of night.
> I dabble in the dapple of the day,
> a heap of wet clothes, seamy, shivering,
> I see my flesh and bedding washed with light,
> my child exploding into dynamite
>
> ("Night Sweat," *SP* 134)

CHAPTER 1

The Fallen Christian

Study me then, you shall lovers be
At the next world, that is, at the next spring:
   For I am every dead thing,
   In whom love wrought new alchemy.
     For his art did express
A quintessence even from nothingness,
From dull privations, and lean emptiness
He ruined me, and I am re-begot
Of absence, darkness, death; things which are not.
               —John Donne

Lowell's triumph in *Lord Weary's Castle* is his capacity to assimilate disparate, contradictory influences and impulses. Unwilling to sacrifice linguistic density in the name of greater accessibility or formal constraint, he grounds the poems in solid narrative and creates a context to support the verbal richness. Lowell had clearly brooded on this problem. In his review of a book by Dylan Thomas, he says, "Great lines are thrown away because they lack a context in which their force can function. . . . If Thomas kept his eye on his object and depended less on his rhetoric, his poems would be better organized and have more to say." [1]

The least facile of poets, Lowell wanted every line to count and worked hard to order his inner chaos. He was distinguished, beginning with the first poem in *Lord Weary's Castle*, by the sheer gravity and raw weight of his material. Lowell had put himself through a crucible of poetic apprenticeship. If he roughed up dulcet meters it was not so much out of animus towards the form itself, but rather frustration that the form could not contain the matter he wanted it to sustain. As Robert Hass says, "Irony, the stresses falling like chains clanking, is very often Robert Lowell's way with meter. . . . The writing seems to accuse not only the fathers but the culture that produced meter and rhyme."[2] Lowell may have thought poetry had to be violent in order to be powerful, and this *thought* may have enabled him to write the kind of poetry that he wrote.

"The Exile's Return" contains some of Lowell's most characteristic gestures, rhythms, images, and themes. The poem is set in a dramatic context—a battle—capable of withstanding the onslaught of Lowell's extreme, highly charged language. The liveliness and panache, in spite of the grimness of the scene, are affirmed by the sound-play, rhyming, and enjambments.

> There mounts in squalls a sort of rusty mire,
> Not ice, not snow, to leaguer the Hôtel
> De Ville, where braced pig-iron dragons grip
> The blizzard to their rigor mortis. A bell
> Grumbles when the reverberations strip
> The thatching from its spire,
> The search-guns click and spit and split up timber
> And nick the slate roofs on the Holstenwall
> Where torn-up tilestones crown the victor. . . .
>
> (*SP* 3)

The verb "mounts" in the first line is strange when combined with the shrug-of-the-shoulders tone of "a sort of rusty mire." This poem contains other elements that crop up often in Lowell's work: the hyphenated words, the harsh rhymes such as "grip"/"strip," and the near overdose of alliteration, assonance, and half rhyme as in the "click and spit and split up timber," slowing you down, almost making you stumble. Lowell has entirely transformed the world (a war-torn landscape) into art here and can get away with anything as long as he stays within his own system. None of the words go together *naturally*.

> Where torn-up tilestones crown the victor. Fall
> And winter, spring and summer, guns unlimber
> And lumber down the narrow gabled street
> Past your gray, sorry and ancestral house
> Where the dynamited walnut tree
> Shadows a squat, old, wind-torn gate and cows
> The Yankee commandant. . . .
>
> (*SP* 3)

The diurnal rotation of the seasons is evoked here as if some kind of normalcy had returned to the world. But this is not the case, for what follows is an image of "guns" that "unlimber/ And lumber down the narrow gabled street." The rhyming of "unlimber" and "timber" softens the "guns" so that we cannot read the verb "lumber" in the next line without also thinking of the noun. These connections are not hidden. Once we recognize this we read the poem with more pleasure than we might have predicted from the bleakness of the scene.

The success of "The Exile's Return," as with many poems to come, hinges on sound: you can't help but hear the cadence of boots, the gun butts striking the pavement, and you see the motorcade of returning soldiers, rolling into the Market Square as in a newsreel.

> The Yankee commandant. You will not see
> Strutting children or meet
> The peg-leg and reproachful chancellor
> With a forget-me-not in his button-hole

When the unseasoned liberators roll
Into the Market Square, ground arms before
The Rathaus; but already lily-stands
Burgeon the risen Rhineland, and a rough
Cathedral lifts its eye. Pleasant enough,
Voi ch'entrate, and your life is in your hands.

(SP 3)

The end of the war signifies return to ordinary life, "and
your life is in your hands." And the end of the poem points to
an uncertain future when the collective psyche will no longer be
able to vent some of its darkest feelings through the guise of a
common cause. The narrator fears "the unseasoned liberators,"
all those conquering heroes, those raw recruits who have not yet
begun to live, more than he fears the "rusty mire" and the backdrop of war and violence and destruction. The allusion to the
inscription Dante sees on the gates of Hell, LASCIATE OGNE
SPERANZA, VOI CH'INTRATE (Abandon every hope, you
who enter),[3] is filled with ominous and sorrowful forebodings,
and underscores Lowell's deep affinity with the condition of exile.

As a conscientious objector Lowell did time in the West
Street Jail during World War II and may have felt exiled at
home in America. He documents this period in his life in a later
poem, "Memories of West Street and Lepke."

I was a fire-breathing Catholic C.O.,
and made my manic statement,
telling off the state and president, and then
sat waiting sentence in the bull pen
beside a Negro boy with curlicues
of marijuana in his hair.

Given a year,
I walked on the roof of the West Street Jail. . . .

("Memories of West Street and Lepke," SP 91–92)

Commenting on "The Exile's Return" at his last reading at
the YMHA in New York on December 8, 1976, Lowell says he

wrote it toward the end of the war, borrowing "from Thomas Mann's Tonio Kröger and it's [about] a German coming back . . . maybe a German Jewish refugee coming back to Germany after it's been blasted to pieces . . . I was very religious then . . . I am still but I hide it . . . then I didn't."[4] In the poem Lowell reimagines Tonio Kröger coming back to the town of his childhood, registering the shock of change. The poem contrasts Mann's turn-of-the-century world where "powerful machine-saws hissed and spat and cut up timber,"[5] with one where "searchguns click and spit and split up timber/ And nick the slate roofs on the Holstenwall/ Where torn-up tilestones crown the victor." As though he were addressing Kröger's (or Mann's) ghost, Lowell shows what has become of "his large, ancestral home . . . the first in all the town . . . Holstenwall . . . the old walnut tree."[6] All have been defiled by force and violence.

The tone of Mann's story is quiet in comparison to "The Exile's Return." The poem mirrors the change in consciousness after the two World Wars. Reading *Tonio Kröger* along with "The Exile's Return" we can see the extent of Lowell's "borrowing." He uses some of the key images in Mann's story as fixed points, pivots for his "story," in order to ground his imagination. He even rewrites lines from H. T. Lowe-Porter's translation, but he intensifies the language and makes the setting more grotesque. Compare the second sentence of the story, "There came in gusts a sort of soft hail, not ice, not snow,"[7] with the opening lines of the poem, "There mounts in squalls a sort of rusty mire,/ Not ice, not snow."

Many of Lowell's poems are adaptations of literary and other texts. This is an age-old tradition, in keeping with the spirit of his "favorite English poetry . . . the difficult Elizabethan plays and the Metaphysicals" (*PRI* 356). Commenting on Webster's plays, D. C. Gunby writes:

The technique he employed was the standard one of his age—an age, it should be remembered, when no stigma attached to what is now called plagiarism, when on the contrary rhetorical tradition encouraged imitation. . . . To emphasize Webster's borrowing, it should be stressed, is not to decry his artistry. On the contrary, what he borrowed he generally bettered by reworking, and always made his own.[8]

So did Lowell. And so did Shakespeare. The material was there to be used. We are not disappointed to discover that Prospero's grand address in *The Tempest*, "Ye elves of hills, brooks, standing lakes, and groves," is derived from Golding's translation of Ovid's *Metamorphoses*, "Ye airs and winds, ye elves of hills, of brooks, of woods alone."[9]

Lowell began writing poetry during the heyday of "modernism," when Pound and Eliot were at the peak of their influence and Williams was finally gaining much delayed recognition. They set the standard that Lowell tried to meet. Some of the things we find in "The Exile's Return" which seem like outrageous gestures are merely standard stylistic ingredients of modernist poetry: quotation/allusion ("*Voi ch'entrate*"); the use of a hidden persona (Tonio Kröger); commentary, often portentous, on "the times." Eliot's *The Waste Land* was then read as a tract on the decline and fall of Western civilization, not as disguised autobiography. *Lord Weary's Castle*, as well as being an apocalyptic book and a book of negative prophecies, marks the end of this tradition in American poetry.

Let's take another look at the beginning of "The Exile's Return"—"There mounts in squalls a sort of rusty mire." Here, as in many of Lowell's poems, the opening line leads into a determined world—the frame is set, something is astir, our curiosity is piqued. This initial image stays with us, sticks in our mind.

In this context, "mounts," a highly charged and suggestive verb, adds sexual tension to a line about the weather, especially in light of the "unseasoned liberators" yet to come. This, combined with the "rusty mire," suggests the vanishing of artillery fire, the utter destruction of the city with its "dynamited walnut tree." The emotional pressure behind these lines is so strong that even the extremity of the setting can barely contain it. There are scores of bad war poems. But this poem works precisely because it successfully projects the poet's internal conflicts.

At the time, Lowell was trying to write a certain *kind* of poem. Years later he reflected playfully on this early poetry, "I was . . . reading Hart Crane and Thomas and Tate and Empson's *Seven Types of Ambiguity;* and each poem was more difficult than the one before, and had more ambiguities" (*PRI* 341). Empson—echoing Richards and Eliot—focused attention on the difficult poetry of the sixteenth and seventeenth centuries, particularly Shakespeare of the late tragedies and such "metaphysicals" as Donne and Vaughn. Lowell was well aware of an ideal of language and style typified by the standards Empson defined. Yet one of the problems—the Pandora's Box Empson opened—was the undiscriminating "interpretation" of ambiguities: as if context did not matter, or as if one word could change context itself.

Linguistic density and directness are difficult to meld. Lowell's poetry is so forthright in tone; the poems grab your attention with things that seem to be *there* before we become aware through such devices as enjambment ("Hôtel/De Ville") that he intends us to know that words reconstitute the world. Lowell gives the concrete illusion of realism, but I think that subject matter for him is the sieve through which the materials of the medium have to flow. He relies on the visible world to the extent to which he can forget it, banish its presence through its recreation in words that grapple with the nature of seeing and perceiving, with the artist as the medium, seer. There is almost no photography in Lowell's poetry. He never merely describes.

꿍뀷

Lowell manages to gather tremendous tension and rivets it to the welter of things which range through his poems. The tension doesn't seek release; it seeks extermination, conflagration, upheaval, roiling turmoil. Nowhere is this more evident than in "The Quaker Graveyard in Nantucket," a long poem by modern standards but exceedingly condensed. Lowell seemed to want to write another *Moby Dick* in 143 lines. The poem has seven sections, with the sixth, "Our Lady of Walsingham," standing at a tangent to the rest, giving respite, reprieve. "The Quaker Graveyard in Nantucket" is a controlled, extended synapse, where the imagination is so engaged by the action that it cannot pause; and yet however furious the hush behind the lines, the blankness behind the matter, the language can overstep the bounds of caution and closed-couplet civility (which for Lowell would have been servility) because the poem must have existed in imagination beforehand as, in the deepest sense, preverbal experience.

The title itself, "The Quaker Graveyard in Nantucket (for Warren Winslow, Dead at Sea)," brings with it some definite echoes. We are immediately reminded of two other poems in the elegiac tradition: Milton's "Lycidas" dedicated to Edward King, another drowned man, and Shelley's "Adonais." Lowell was always quick to appropriate great subjects from the tradition. This layering of vision, going beyond the individual mourned, is designated by the genre. I think he needed this ballast, these poetic/historical conceits and constraints in order to let go of himself. Within the genre, there he feels free.

The graveyard, the presence of death therein, the drowned man, the fact that the men are Quakers—these are some of the integers that stir his imagination. The death in the poem is also his own. He comes as close as a man can to imagining his own death.

The first three sections of the poem focus on the human drama. The common theme is death by drowning: the death of the drowned sailor, the death of Ahab, and the death of the whale are paralleled. The next two sections focus on the wounded whale and the micro- and macrocosmic repercussions of its traumatic death. The sailors and the whale are bound together as victor and victim and neither can escape annihilation. The sixth section explores the possibility of grace through penitence and provides the only glimmer of hope. At the center of the last section the ocean itself, the "old mouth of the Atlantic"—a harsh, impartial element—dissolves the dialectic of the poem.

The poem begins:

> A brackish reach of shoal off Madaket—
> The sea was still breaking violently and night
> Had steamed into our North Atlantic Fleet,
> When the drowned sailor clutched the drag-net. Light

(*SP* 6)

Poems should be read as they were written, in the context of habitat, with full attention paid to the spirit of place. So much of this poem is listening, hearing the roar of the ocean behind the first line, audible but invisible. The indefinite article works to give us a sense of the vast space he wants to encompass, compress. The line resounds clangingly like a chain dropped on the rocky shore. Nothing could be more direct and yet by the time we "reach" the dash that propels us into the second line, what do we have, where are we? We think we know because Madaket can be found on any map of Nantucket, but the place is intangible because the line refers to the "brackish reach of shoal" which, like the true content of the poem, is underwater, a threat to sailors. All in all a good beginning for a poem about a shipwreck. And it does what a first line should do: draws you into the poem, hurls you into the second line by its rapidity.

> The sea was still breaking violently and night

"Still" adds an extra syllable to the line and breaks its rhythm. Without it the line would be merely descriptive. The anapest "was still break—" arrests our attention and thrusts us into the eternal present.

> The presence of genius is not shown in elaborating a picture: we have had many specimens of this sort of work in modern poems, where all is so dutchified, if I may use the word, by the most minute touches, that the reader naturally asks why words, and not painting, are used.
>
> The power of poetry is, by a single word perhaps, to instill that energy into the mind which compels the imagination to produce the picture.[10]

In the opening lines of "The Quaker Graveyard" Lowell does what Coleridge indirectly admonished poets to do: he creates a dialogue between historical and mythological time without diverging from the narrative.

Still, still, still. Whenever Lowell uses the word "still" we know that something is about to change, if not for the character in the poem, then for the poet. "Still" connotes a cross between persistence and despair. The dual meanings of the word seem to be at loggerheads.

The sea was still breaking violently
    ("The Quaker Graveyard in Nantucket," *SP* 6)

only Mother, still her Father's daughter.
Her voice was still electric
    ("Commander Lowell," *SP* 76)

Nautilus Island's hermit
heiress still lives through winter in her Spartan cottage;
her sheep still graze above the sea.
    ("Skunk Hour," *SP* 95)

clearest of all God's creatures, still all air and nerve:
    ("Man and Wife," *SP* 93)

Still over us, still in parenthesis,
    ("New York 1962: Fragment," *SP* 132)

still watch their crippled last survivors pass,
    ("The Neo-Classical Urn," *SP* 126)

His vision was still twenty-twenty.
    ("Terminal Days at Beverly Farms," *SP* 80)

still unbelieving, unconfessed and unreceived,
    ("For George Santayana," *SP* 61)

"I'm still twenty, I've done badly, I'll do better."
    ("Saint-Just 1767–93," *SP* 171)

to the God of our fathers still twenty like themselves.
    ("Verdun," *SP* 175)

Randall, the scene still plunges at the windshield,
    ("Randall Jarrell 1. October 1965," *SP* 177)

    the rapid young
still brand your hand with sunflecks . . .
    ("For Eugene McCarthy," *SP* 182)

a limb that weighed a ton
still shakes green leaves
    ("We Took Our Paradise," *DBD* 57)

still air expiring from the tilting bubble—
    ("1930's," *SP* 189)

the sun stockstill like Joshua's in midfield
("Long Summers," *SP* 191)

still had her Freudian papá and maids!
("During Fever," *SP* 86)

My hand draws back. I often sigh still
("For the Union Dead," *SP* 135)

Lowell establishes the tone of "The Quaker Graveyard in Nantucket" so surely, grounds it so forcibly in the world, that he is able to turn nature and the elements into active agents which compel us to receive the fourth line without shock: it's almost a relief from the tension that has been building in the scene. The details of what ensues have the vivid precision of a nightmare. Time is suspended. The corpse, rising to the surface, becomes more and more clarified.

> When the drowned sailor clutched the drag-net. Light
> Flashed from his matted head and marble feet,
> He grappled at the net
> With the coiled, hurdling muscles of his thighs:
> The corpse was bloodless, a botch of reds and whites,
> Its open, staring eyes
> Were lustreless dead-lights
> Or cabin-windows on a stranded hulk
> Heavy with sand.
>
> (*SP* 6)

Lowell learned from Milton the effect of the shortened line in a basically set pattern of iambic pentameter. He uses it here to reenact the drowning as if he could parry the fact that the sailor is already dead ("He grappled at the net . . ."). The bloodless corpse that emerges looks like it has been underwater for a long time. The landscape has receded. The corpse is returned to its watery grave, fed to the sharks, herded back to the deeps.

> We weight the body, close
> Its eyes and heave it seaward whence it came,
> Where the heel-headed dogfish barks its nose
> On Ahab's void and forehead;

Note the black comedy of Lowell's puns: this dog is no god; it mocks Ahab's fear of the void, symbolized in Moby Dick's forehead, by barking its nose. Lowell treats Ahab, the *Pequod*, and Moby Dick as if they had historical reality; life and literature intersect. Even the lines "ask for no Orphean lute/ To pluck life back" have a gorgeous doubleness. To show that the world has changed irrevocably since the time when Milton in "Lycidas" could use the image of Orpheus as a genuine source of inspiration, Lowell moves directly from the impossible lute to say

> The guns of the steeled fleet
> Recoil and then repeat
> The hoarse salute.

Lowell rejects the stance of nostalgia; yet the lyrical beauty survives. And now through the sounds of the warships we hear the harsh reverberations of modern war and become painfully aware that we are in World War II.

Section II, addressed to his cousin Warren Winslow, is a beautiful, excruciating prayer, conducted by the elements.

> Whenever winds are moving and their breath
> Heaves at the roped-in bulwarks of this pier,
> The terns and sea-gulls tremble at your death
> In these home waters. . . .

> Sea-gulls blink their heavy lids
> Seaward. The winds' wings beat upon the stones,
> Cousin, and scream for you and the claws rush
> At the sea's throat and wring it in the slush
> Of this old Quaker graveyard where the bones
> Cry out in the long night for the hurt beast
> Bobbing by Ahab's whaleboats in the East.

These are among the most realized lines in the poem: the former for the sensitivity with which they register the reaction in nature to this untimely death and the deftness of the self-projection outward into the world; the latter for sheer momentum. The deeper Lowell plunges into the sadness these thoughts of death have brought him, the more alert he becomes. He rivets our attention to the heavy eyelids of the seagulls. He makes us visualize them perched on the shaky bulwarks in that stop-time moment before they take flight. It is their departure and the beating of their invisible wings that make it possible, suddenly, for the language to become more metaphorical and the "winds' wings [to] beat upon the stones . . . and scream."

Section III is a meditation on American history. Lowell contrasts the violence of "our warships,"

> Guns, cradled on the tide,
> Blast the eelgrass about a waterclock
> Of bilge and backwash, roil the salt and sand
> Lashing earth's scaffold . . .

with the innocence and stoicism of the Quaker sailors. In the moment when he witnesses their death he is, as it were, pierced by compassion.

> Whatever it was these Quaker sailors lost
> In the mad scramble of their lives. They died
> When time was open-eyed,
> Wooden and childish; only bones abide
> There, in the nowhere, where their boats were tossed
> Sky-high, where mariners had fabled news
> Of IS, the whited monster. What it cost
> Them is their secret. In the sperm-whale's slick
> I see the Quakers drown and hear their cry:
> "If God himself had not been on our side,
> If God himself had not been on our side,
> When the Atlantic rose against us, why,
> Then it had swallowed us up quick."

These last four lines have the tone of early American sermons by Jonathan Edwards or Cotton Mather and the simplicity and vigor of a ballad like "Thomas Rhymer":

> For forty days and forty nights
> He wade thro red blude to the knee,
> And he saw neither sun nor moon,
> But heard the roaring of the sea.

The ocean of Lowell's poem isn't unbounded. We have the sense that America, through its power, had begun to dominate the sea the way she came to dominate the world. The Quaker sailors who died when time was "open-eyed,/ Wooden and childish" didn't have to face the transformation of America into an instrument of force.

Ahab is used as a figure throughout the poem, for Lowell shares with Ahab his monomania and his desire to strike through the "pasteboard masks." He has the same restlessness and tension, which cannot be relieved by anything on earth. The annihilation of the whale cannot be enacted without the concomitant death of the self. Ahab had to die to kill his own pain and Lowell uses this death in his poem as an omen. Because Lowell's conflicts are insoluble, his vision is tragic. No worldly resolution is possible. He judges and is judged by an implacable, if absent and unanswering, God.

More and more in "The Quaker Graveyard in Nantucket" we come to feel that we're in a capsule of projected space, a cork-lined echo chamber, and that the action is the action of Lowell's mind made sensible to us through the physicality of the language and the complexity of the form. The stanzaic designs he uses in this poem are as complicated and rigid as those in any formal stanza pattern (Italian sonnet, Spenserian stanza, *ottava rima*, ballad). In Section IV it is an inventive ten-line stanza with a truncated sixth line and a well-defined rhyme scheme (a,b,c,b,c,a,a,c′,c′,a in the first and a,b,c,b,c,a,d,e,e,d in the second). In the first stanza the headlong run-on lines, all ending on *l* sounds, gather into sound-chords that echo some submerged trauma culminating in the *rime riche*—"whale"/"wail." Into the maelstrom.

> This is the end of the whaleroad and the whale
> Who spewed Nantucket bones on the thrashed swell
> And stirred the troubled waters to whirlpools
> To send the Pequod packing off to hell:
> This is the end of them, three-quarters fools,
> Snatching at straws to sail
> Seaward and seaward on the turntail whale,
> Spouting out blood and water as it rolls,
> Sick as a dog to these Atlantic shoals:
> *Clamavimus,* O depths. Let the sea-gulls wail
>
> For water, for the deep where the high tide
> Mutters to its hurt self, mutters and ebbs.
> Waves wallow in their wash, go out and out,
> Leave only the death-rattle of the crabs,
> The beach increasing, its enormous snout
> Sucking the ocean's side.

Up until this point the poem has affected a narrative. This is the moment when the switchover occurs: the moment before catharsis, release. Lowell has more compassion for Ahab and the whale than for the drowned sailor. We pity the whale ("Pity the monsters!" Lowell exclaims in "Florence," a later poem, *SP* 107), but the drowned sailor is made lurid and grotesque. It is always necessary to consider Lowell's attitude toward his subjects, since the subjects themselves are so much a part of the literary repertory; it's his radical variations on these themes, the havoc he wreaks on them, that draws us to him. And in "The Quaker Graveyard in Nantucket," one word stands out above all others—death—no matter how it comes.

> When the whale's viscera go and the roll
> Of its corruption overruns this world

> Beyond tree-swept Nantucket and Woods Hole
> And Martha's Vineyard, Sailor, will your sword
> Whistle and fall and sink into the fat?

There is a pattern in Lowell's best poems that I can identify here. By the end of "Memories of West Street and Lepke," for instance, after his imagination has completed its trajectory, Lowell *becomes* Lepke; in "The Quaker Graveyard" he becomes the whale—who is so brutally butchered in Section V. He becomes the whale because he can't appease the guilt he feels for what men have done to it. This is one way "I" becomes "another." Without ceasing to be an elegy, the poem starts to question the repercussions of a life. Lowell recognizes what his heritage has become and finds in the butchering of the whale a symbol for all of America's (and the world's) mindless brutality. He finds it intolerable, as does Melville, and unleashes a fury of indignation back at the destroyers. This, after all, is the same Robert Lowell who told off the state and president. And perhaps, as a Lowell, he felt his words could influence the world. What's madness but omnipotence of thought, or as his friend Roethke put it, "nobility of soul at odds with circumstance." Some of the poem's power comes from Lowell's pride in America and his hatred of its violence. Lowell's pacifism wasn't empty rhetoric: he paid for it.

In this poem it is as if the collective past, or the accumulated noise of history, gathering in that instant, exists, now, like the sea, to devour us. Death, through the bones of those who have already died, sucks us backwards, sucks the life force out of us.

> In the great ash-pit of Jehoshaphat
> The bones cry for the blood of the white whale,
> The fat flukes arch and whack about its ears,
> The death-lance churns into the sanctuary, tears

The gun-blue swingle, heaving like a flail,
And hacks the coiling life out: it works and drags
And rips the sperm-whale's midriff into rags,
Gobbets of blubber spill to wind and weather,
Sailor, and gulls go round the stoven timbers
Where the morning stars sing out together
And thunder shakes the white surf and dismembers
The red flag hammered in the mast-head. Hide,
Our steel, Jonas Messias, in Thy side.

It's an astonishing idea actually, that death lives and lives only
to devour what is alive, and that the life force is nothing in
comparison to this death energy, this vortex in chorus: "Where
the morning stars sing out together/ And thunder shakes the
white surf and dismembers/ The red flag hammered in the mast-
head." Ripping a paraphrase from Job 38:7 out of context to
emphasize how far we have fallen ("When the morning-stars sang
together, *and all the sons of God shouted for joy?*"; italics mine),
Lowell accuses us, mankind, of shredding and dismembering
God's creation. Then by joining Jonah and the Messiah he creates a complex symbol of death and rebirth. "Hide,/ Our steel,
Jonas Messias, in Thy side," but his guilt is an afterthought to
the primary feeling.

After this passage Lowell has to speak at a tangent to direct
us to the core of his concern. Before, he plied the language toward its limits, via description and physicality; now, searching
for a hiatus from the violence, he takes a meditative turn and
starts to imagine himself out of hell or out of the hell of his
imagination.

"Our Lady of Walsingham" is the most surprising section
of the poem. The shift of tone is more startling (but gently,
gently) than the image of the drowned sailor clutching the drag-
net. The key phrase in the first stanza—before the Lady en-

ters—is "lose/ Track of your dragging pain." But to get there and beyond his source[11] he needs his "munching English lane."

> There once the penitents took off their shoes
> And then walked barefoot the remaining mile;
> And the small trees, a stream and hedgerows file
> Slowly along the munching English lane,
> Like cows to the old shrine, until you lose
> Track of your dragging pain.
> The stream flows down under the druid tree,
> Shiloah's whirlpools gurgle and make glad
> The castle of God. Sailor, you were glad
> And whistled Sion by that stream. But see:

Notice the twist in the injunction. In a poem that has had everything invested in seeing, Lowell has never asked us to look at anything. Until now, when he leans toward Grace.

> Our Lady, too small for her canopy,
> Sits near the altar. There's no comeliness
> At all or charm in that expressionless
> Face with its heavy eyelids. As before,
> This face, for centuries a memory,
> *Non est species, neque decor,*
> Expressionless, expresses God: it goes
> Past castled Sion. She knows what God knows,
> Not Calvary's Cross nor crib at Bethlehem
> Now, and the world shall come to Walsingham.

The use of the Latin phrase ("There is no ostentation, nor elegance") makes us aware of her changeless presence. For centuries the shrine had been a historical site; and in this passage Lowell reestablishes her image as an object of worship.

Nowhere is the direct lineage from Eliot to Lowell more evident than in the last line. It echoes *Four Quartets* ("in a secluded chapel/ History is now and England"[12]), which Lowell had reviewed with the fervor of one who aspires to another state of being:

> My own feeling is that *union with God* is somewhere in sight in
> all poetry, though it is usually rudimentary and misunder-
> stood. . . . Probably the contemplative's life, as distinguished
> from his separate acts, can only be dramatized by a circular and
> thematic structure. His actions, unlike the tragic hero's, have no
> beginning, middle or end: their external unity is a pawn to their
> unity of intention.[13]

Again, the lack of dramatic differentiation is mimetically realized in rhythm. And "union with God" is arrived at or reached
for through rituals of repetition: through rocking rhythm, and
the forms of tradition. Crossing the boundaries of tradition and
genre can be a symbolic form of communion with God (entering
the temple of form to cross the lines into the saved, taking the
veil to take off the veil). Lowell's evocation of "Our Lady" also
closely parallels Eliot's invocation to the "Lady" in *Ash Wednesday*. These poems are gestures toward transcendence, ways of
finding a path through hell. The crucial difference is that Eliot,
through the poems themselves, is seeking a state of spiritual grace,
release from worldly tensions ("Teach us to care and not to
care"[14]), whereas Lowell is trying to force "an entrance" (*I* 116,
Montale, "The Coastguard House") into life, to fall into time—
"and the world shall come to Walsingham." Eliot can approach
the "Lady" in *Ash Wednesday* because he believes in her and because he has renounced "the blessèd face"[15] and has to "construct something/ Upon which to rejoice."[16] Eliot's text explains
how the face of Lowell's "Lady" "Expressionless, expresses God":

> Because of the goodness of this Lady
> And because of her loveliness, and because
> She honours the Virgin in meditation,
> We shine with brightness. . . .[17]

Eliot, in *Ash Wednesday*, is Lowell's Vergil, his spiritual—
not his formal—precursor. But Eliot seems to me an authentic
convert. Religion was not something he grabbed onto in desper-

ation to keep himself from sinking. Lowell's need to lose track
of his "dragging pain," his puritanical shackles, may have drawn
him to Catholicism, but neither God nor the sea would ever
become a haven for his imagination. He would never know grace
or ease or release from his sense of burden. Twenty years later—
and no longer a Catholic—he would have Endecott, in his dram-
atization of Hawthorne's story "Endecott and the Red Cross,"
voice the same desperation: "I feel ridiculous,/ standing here en-
closed in iron. . . . If I could crawl out of my armor . . . I
might be alive then. . . . Look, I am the hollowness inside my
armor" (*OG* 40, 41). He would never *transcend*. He could only
hear the furious onrush of the waves, "where the high tide/ Mutters to its hurt self, mutters and ebbs" (*SP* 8). Lowell is attuned
mainly to the harshness of the sea, its brutality, but "The Quaker
Graveyard" works aesthetically because his imagination is married to the Atlantic and the barren, rugged Nantucket landscape, where living things must buffet wind and sea to survive.

In the final section of the poem Lowell makes audible the
creaking that we heard behind the lines that began the second
stanza. Compare:

> Whenever winds are moving and their breath
> Heaves at the roped-in bulwarks of this pier
>
> (Section II, *SP* 7)

with:

> The empty winds are creaking and the oak
> Splatters and splatters on the cenotaph
>
> (Section VII, *SP* 10)

The language is plainer, coming after "Our Lady of Walsingham." In a way he turns the poem on its head, forging affir-
mation out of negation. He moves from the cemetery out to sea
where Warren Winslow's body is buried,

                              and a gaff
            Bobs on the untimely stroke
            Of the greased wash exploding on a shoal-bell
            In the old mouth of the Atlantic. It's well;
            Atlantic, you are fouled with the blue sailors,
            Sea-monsters, upward angel, downward fish:
            Unmarried and corroding, spare of flesh

The syntax of these lines is complex and the key phrase is the
one that pertains least to the action: "Unmarried and corroding."
Lowell may have been thinking primarily of his cousin and all
the other young sailors who died with him. There is also a *tone*
to the passage that links the Atlantic to the Lord God, himself
"unmarried."

There is no life force without a death force. Lowell, in
keeping with his Biblical sources, is unrelenting on this issue.
He holds fast to the doubleness, as

            When the Lord God formed man from the sea's slime
            And breathed into his face the breath of life,
            And blue-lung'd combers lumbered to the kill.
            The Lord survives the rainbow of His will.

In this poem, ripe with ambiguities, there is a point of clarity:
the human element. It is our dominion, our place in the order
of things, that we abuse and God withdraws, according to Lowell, in the last line of the poem.

"The Quaker Graveyard in Nantucket" can be viewed as a
paradigm for how his imagination works. There's no "I," no ego
in the poem. Lowell becomes what he beholds, the perceiver
perceived. His hatred for and anger towards the Puritans for
their killing of the whale combine with his subliminal identification with their action—which he condemns. Lowell was a Puritan, it was part of his heritage, it was in his bones so the hatred
is also self-hatred, which accounts for the violence of the dis-

memberment "When the whale's viscera go and the roll/ Of its corruption overruns this world."

But this is also a love poem to the white whale. If Lowell identifies with the pain of anyone or anything in the poem it is with that of the whale. Yet we could apply Lowell's warning in "Epics" about reading too much meaning into *Moby Dick* to the poem because it, too, is "fiction, not history" and like *Moby Dick* it also "tells us not to break our necks on a brick wall." In *Moby Dick* Ahab half-recognizes that he sought out his own destruction, more than it had sought him. Despite his monomania, Ahab lives at the pitch of ambivalence. The same fierce ambivalence gives "The Quaker Graveyard in Nantucket" its lasting fascination. If the whale could "send the Pequod packing off to hell" then think what the ocean could do to the fragile human settlement, Nantucket. The violence is not Lowell's conjuration here; it isn't willed or used for effect. He mourns his cousin, Warren Winslow, as best he can, yet cannot recoil, turn his gaze away from the unseemly paradoxes of the voyage: the Puritans' rage against the elements, their willingness to conquer nature, their absence of ambivalence, for which they are culpable. All of the Puritan's heretofore repressed violence is unleashed at the whale. There are no easy distinctions, no one motive. As Lowell said some thirty years after the poem was written:

> A poem changes with each inspection. Variability is its public existence. Yet variety has limits; no one could call *Macbeth* or my *Quaker Graveyard* hilarious minuets. That would take an insensately amusing theorist.[18]

Lowell turns the Emersonian "overall" upside down, reinforcing all the pain and unappeasable sadness in the poem. There is, literally, a synthesis ("The Lord survives the rainbow of His will"), however grim, and the Atlantic dissolves the dialectic. And the sadness has weight because Lowell would always find

the essential conflicts irreconcilable in his life and the resulting
tension would often come to overwhelm him.

❧

We have to keep in mind that Lowell was a Lowell, one of
New England's patrician families, a fact, as Elizabeth Bishop
observed, that may have given him a certain confidence which
is reflected in his writing as well as his life. Although the question of ancestry and biography are outside the scope of this project we can find in it some of the sources of Lowell's ambivalence, certainly the defining characteristic of his poetry.

His parents' marriage was a merger of two eminent Boston-
ian families. His mother, Charlotte Winslow Lowell, was a de-
scendant of Edward Winslow, who came to America on the
Mayflower, Josiah Winslow, the Governor of Plymouth Colony
(and renowned Indian killer), and John Stark, Revolutionary War
General. The ancestors of his father, Commander Robert Traill
Spence Lowell, were better known for intellectual endeavors.
Among them were Robert Traill Spence Lowell, Episcopal rec-
tor and the headmaster of St. Mark's School, the noted astron-
omer Percival Lowell, Abbot Lawrence Lowell, the President of
Harvard, James Russell Lowell, poet, professor, and Ambassa-
dor to England, and Amy Lowell, poet and standard-bearer of
the imagist movement.

If the Winslows could be said to represent the active side
of Lowell's nature, the Lowells could be said to represent the
intellectual and artistic side. Perhaps young Robert felt most alive
when engaged in the spirit of rebellion, making manic statements, crying out against loneliness and injustice and the fact of
death. He was the wild boy who knocks over all of the bric-a-
brac, who loves to make an effect. The only solution to an in-

soluble problem is for him to become an artist. So he says to his family, in essence, I will not be like you, and opens up the realm of negation. I will not—.

It must have been a blow to his family when he left Harvard for Kenyon College, and one can imagine their response when he converted to Catholicism just prior to his marriage to Jean Stafford. In 1943, when Lowell declared himself a conscientious objector, his action was greeted by an article in the *New York Times* (October 12, 1943), "A 'Boston Lowell' Is a Draft Dodger." This attention was a result of his lineage, not his poetry, which was not well known enough at the time to warrant this public response. But in 1965 when, to protest U.S. involvement in Vietnam, he declined President Johnson's invitation to a White House Festival on the Arts, his letter was printed on the front page of the *New York Times*, and Johnson was enraged.

Strange as it may seem, it was liberating for Lowell to become a Catholic. It gave him a sense of ritual and tradition missing from Episcopalianism (the church of "society" in the East). Catholicism allowed him an outlet for his violence and his ever-present need to be bloody and civilized at the same time. And becoming Catholic had social as well as religious repercussions for him because he aligned himself with the Irish working class.

If, because of his name, Lowell was part of American history then does it follow that everything he did would become part of that history? No. He earned his way through the coalescence of talent (primarily that), and will. Look at the other Lowells, James Russell and Amy, whose poetry is mainly of historical interest, and look at Lowell's father, the Commander.

This is what Lowell had to say about the importance of his lineage to his development as a writer:

I never knew I was a Lowell till I was twenty. The ancestors known to my family were James Russell Lowell, a poet pedestalled for oblivion, and no asset to his grandnephew among the rich athletes at boarding school. Another, my great-grandfather, James Russell's brother, had been headmaster of my boarding school, and left a memory of scholarly aloofness. He wrote an ironic Trollopian *roman à clef* about the school. There was Amy Lowell, big and a scandal, as if Mae West were a cousin. And there were rich Lowells, but none as rich as classmates' grandfathers in New York. Of course, we were flesh and blood, but I am talking down rumors of our grandeur. My immediate family, if you have an English equivalent, would be the Duke of Something's sixth cousins. We gave no feeling of swagger. Later I felt a blood kinship with James Russell's savage vernacular anti-Mexican way and pro-Civil War *Bigelow Papers*—they were not for the thirties. Was Amy a rebel artist or an entrepreneur? Ours was an old family. It stood—just. Its last eminence was Lawrence, Amy's brother, and president of Harvard for millennia, a grand *fin de siècle* president, a species long dead in America. He was cultured in the culture of 1900—very deaf, very sprightly, in his eighties. He was unique in our family for being able to read certain kinds of good poetry. I used to spend evenings with him, and go home to college at four in the morning.[19]

Lowell inherited aspects of a sensibility as well as a name. As a child Robert loved to say "No"—"I won't go with you. I want to stay with Grandpa!" ("My Last Afternoon with Uncle Devereux Winslow," *SP* 66) as if to say, I want to feel my way back in time through history, to touch—the source—to feel, as Paula Modersohn-Becker put it, "the gentle vibration of things," the quick of being. And the stress Lowell felt in living and always going against the grain is evident even in his meters—he resists and stretches—but is rarely willing to be without the boundary of fixed forms. Lowell always acted with the supposition that he was standing for something ("It seems I am choosing words that will stand, . . . but if I blunder, it doesn't matter—I must persist in my errors" ("For Anna Akhmatova," Pasternak, [*I*, p. 133]) and his acts, his private frames of reference, did find their way into the public domain. Lowell felt he could be a poetic mouthpiece for America and it is this tone that led Richard Poirier to call him "our truest historian." On the other hand, Lowell thought much of his heritage was a trap. His conflicted feelings toward his family are a steady undercurrent of his work. He writes with such a vengeance. It is as if he were attempting to rescue, wrest, his own identity from the complex of the Lowell heritage. His feeling of blood kinship with James Russell is interesting, as we can see, especially in light of Henry James' description of Lowell's great-granduncle. (James and the elder Lowell became close friends when both were Americans abroad.) According to Leon Edel,

> [James Russell] Lowell was a homespun Yankee, a lover of the American vernacular who also vastly preferred Cambridge to the Champs Élysées. Henry perhaps remembered this when he spoke of him as having "the simplicity as of childhood or of Brattle Street." His weak point, Henry wrote to William that autumn, would always be his opinions. His strong point, we may judge, for Henry at least, was that he was the American of his time "most saturated with literature and most directed to criticism." Henry thought his poetry to be that of the outraged citizen smiting a lyre, rather than the poetry of the addicted artist; and he smiled gently on Lowell's pugnacious parochialism. [20]

Young Lowell must have known in his bones that he, too, had an inclination to sermonize, and his formal mastery was in some ways an answer to it.

❧❦❧

    Five of Lowell's important poems of this period—"Between the Porch and the Altar," "After the Surprising Conversions," "Falling Asleep over the Aeneid," "Mother Marie Therese," and "Thanksgiving's Over"—are dramatic monologues in couplets modeled on Browning.

The couplet I've used is very much like the couplet Browning uses in "My Last Duchess," in *Sordello,* run-on with its rhymes buried. I've always, when I've used it, tried to give the impression that I had as much freedom in choosing the rhyme word as I had in any of the other words. Yet they were almost all true rhymes, and maybe half the time there'd be a pause after the rhyme. I wanted something as fluid as prose; you wouldn't notice the form, yet looking back you'd find that great obstacles had been climbed.

(PRI 344)

"Between the Porch and the Altar" is the pivotal poem in *Lord Weary's Castle.* It would even be an appropriate subtitle, given its concerns, revealed in the titles of the four sections: "Mother and Son"; "Adam and Eve"; "Katherine's Dream"; and "At the Altar." The poem reenacts the torment of every man's fall. Both here and in "The Quaker Graveyard in Nantucket" Lowell relies heavily on the first chapter of Genesis. Yet it is strange to refer to him—even during this period—as a religious poet.

"Between the Porch and the Altar" looks forward to Lowell's later works because the suffering in the poem is caused by the parents and family of the protagonists, and not by Lucifer. By this time Freudian theory had permeated every level of culture, from Jimmy Cagney's mother-dominated gangster in *White Heat* to Arshile Gorky's successive portraits of *The Artist and His Mother.* Ernest Jones' *Hamlet and Oedipus* provided another inroad into the universal and still undisclosed (that is, "repressed") potency of this primal material. Lowell hits you right between the eyes with his conflicts and complexes. He makes the latent content manifest by placing the family romance in the foreground of his narratives, and at the same time eschewing "depth," attending to surfaces to keep the reader's disbelief suspended by the plot.

And if Lowell's friends at the *Partisan Review* were applying

brews of Marx and Freud to their criticism, Lowell mixed Freud
and the Bible. But how different was this highly conscious use
of the unconscious from the work done by Proust, Joyce, Eliot,
and Faulkner in the early part of the century when literature,
the visual arts, science and psychology were working instinc-
tively along parallel lines.

Lowell discovers in the process of adapting and exploring
ancient Greek and Biblical themes (Oedipus, Adam and Eve,
Electra) that the complexity of his conflicting feelings could
never be resolved. He uses religious and psychological frame-
works to give the poems the cohesion they desperately need: the
stories help objectify and give form and structure to the violent
feelings that leave him at cross-purposes. For poets and writers
like Wordsworth and Thoreau nature represented the mother
("mother nature") or the feminine. Instead of taking solace from
nature Lowell imbues it with many of the violent feelings he has
towards his mother—and Others.

> Meeting his mother makes him lose ten years,
> Or is it twenty? Time, no doubt, has ears
> That listen to the swallowed serpent, wound
> Into its bowels, but he thinks no sound
> Is possible before her, he thinks the past
> Is settled. It is honest to hold fast
> Merely to what one sees with one's own eyes
> When the red velvet curves and haunches rise
> To blot him from the pretty driftwood fire's
> Façade of welcome. Then the son retires
> Into the sack and selfhood of the boy
> Who clawed through fallen houses of his Troy,
> Homely and human only when the flames
> Crackle in recollection. Nothing shames
> Him more than this uncoiling, . . .
>
> ("Between the Porch and the Altar," *SP* 15)

"Meeting his mother" triggers a severe regression. The speaker
has held back, "swallowed," repressed his feelings for so long

and, taken by surprise, he responds to her as if she were Medusa. The son is half paralyzed by her presence: "no sound/ Is possible before her." First, she silences him, then tries to entice him, causing him to disappear. He resurfaces, sustained by a mythical boyhood fantasy which in order to repossess he has to *hear* the flames crackling in the hearth, since his mother stands in the way of the fire, blurring his line of vision. He retreats, temporarily, into memory, in order to regain the sense of autonomy that he felt and took refuge in as a boy. His mother is impeding his sense of inner freedom. He cringes and recoils at her aggressive falsity, her serpentine wiles. He feels guilty for not being able to love his mother or his wife—"The painted dragon, a mother and a wife/ With flat glass eyes pushed at him on a stick." And he backtracks, gathering his forces once more to break out of this classical situation. But his mother is not the only domineering presence in the room; his whole heritage resides there in the guise of "her father's portrait . . . Dangling its watch-chain on the Holy Book."

The narrator's problem can be stated this way: if woman is the devouring serpent embodied in "Mother and Son," then how can he love? In Section II Lowell readapts the story of "Adam and Eve," anticipated in the swallowed serpent of the first section, placing it in Puritan New England.

> The farmer sizzles on his shaft all day.
> He is content and centuries away
> From white-hot Concord, and he stands on guard.
> Or is he melting down like sculptured lard?
> His hand is crisp and steady on the plough.
> I quarreled with you, but am happy now
> To while away my life for your unrest
> Of terror. Never to have lived is best;
> Man tasted Eve with death. I taste my wife
> And children while I hold your hands. . . .
>   ["Between the Porch and the Altar," *SP* 16)

The farmer is everything the narrator isn't: single-minded, sublimated, content. That loaded phrase "sizzles on his shaft," with its implication of gruesome determination, fully expresses the narrator's feeling clarified later in the statement, "I eye the statue with an awed contempt." Eve stands between the narrator's mother and his wife. The farmer, like Adam, stands between his father and himself. The narrator's senses tell him one thing and his historical, religious, and intellectual heritage demand of him another. The conflict between these is intolerable and contributes to his state of frenzy and agitation: he cannot get free.

> They lied,
> My cold-eyed seedy fathers when they died,
> Or rather threw their lives away, to fix
> Sterile, forbidding nameplates on the bricks
> Above a kettle. . . .

The power of the rhymes in the couplets quoted above make emphatic the vengeance, firm it up by fixing it, incising it as though in stone. A word is put in place and the next line not only introduces a new rhyming word but pounds that first one in; "They lied," is underscored by "they died." What feels moving *as* you read becomes emblazoned once you have read.

> I knife
> Their names into this elm. What is exempt?
> I eye the statue with an awed contempt
> And see the puritanical façade
> Of the white church that Irish exiles made
> For Patrick—that Colonial from Rome
> Had magicked the charmed serpents from their home,
> As though he were the Piper. Will his breath
> Scorch the red dragon of my nerves to death?

Did Patrick, patron saint of Ireland, trick Lowell into becoming a Catholic, or is he just another link in the chain of figureheads who helped build up the bulwark of sexual repression that brings the lovers to such a pitch of desperation that they are transformed into the serpent of Genesis, condemned to repeat the past.

> When we try to kiss,
> Our eyes are slits and cringing, and we hiss;
> Scales glitter on our bodies as we fall.
> The Farmer melts upon his pedestal.

Even the Farmer, that statue of the idealized Puritan, melts under Lowell's vengeful gaze. Or is sex this threatening because it collapses New England probity?

The whole poem is highlighted, thrown into relief, by "Katherine's Deam." It was, according to Lowell, a real dream: "I found that I shaped it a bit, and cut it, and allegorized it, but still it was a dream someone had had" (*PRI* 344). He stays inside her experience; necessity tempers rhetoric; the tone here is at once more casual and intense than in anything he had done before. The language is vivid, direct, personal, and above all, urgent. Lowell's male counterpart thinks "no sound/ Is possible before her, he thinks the past/ Is settled," where Katherine feels her despair and conveys it through action and sensation. At the beginning of the section she is hung over, tense, and hysterical. The rasping phone dangles off the hook like a snake.

> It must have been a Friday. I could hear
> The top-floor typist's thunder and the beer
> That you had brought in cases hurt my head;
> I'd sent the pillows flying from my bed,
> I hugged my knees together and I gasped.
> The dangling telephone receiver rasped
> Like someone in a dream who cannot stop
> For breath or logic till his victim drop
> To darkness and the sheets. I must have slept,
> But still could hear my father who had kept
> Your guilty presents but cut off my hair.

For once Lowell is not "working up" the material, though he does weave in a neat Empsonian pun on presence. And the feelings behind the poem, the fear of punishment for sexual misconduct, the breaking of taboos, the loneliness of sudden isolation from God ("You were with me and are gone"), are actualized in imagination, not rhetorical and willed. The familial and religious conflicts of Katherine and the unnamed narrator mirror each other; her struggle is with her father who blackmails her emotionally. The father punishes her but won't take responsibility for his own vindictiveness or jealousy.

> He whispers that he really doesn't care
> If I am your kept woman all my life,
> Or ruin your two children and your wife;
> But my dishonor makes him drink. . . .

"Katherine's Dream" moves from macabre irony to the searing ending that makes me sit bolt upright in my chair.

> I run about in circles till I drop
> Against a padlocked bulkhead in a yard
> Where faces redden and the snow is hard.

Katherine is then transformed into the dancer in the final section who uses her sexuality to excite others rather than turning it back on herself.

In "At the Altar" the narrator remains detached and physically passive, hoping to heal himself through his eyes, fixing his gaze on the dancer's skate, until it simulates the hypnotic green beacons of the northern lights, to cut himself loose from all this. The "I" is the "he" of Section I. And although this section is in the first person, the language is tightly wound and the tone is heightened and the individual details are out of proportion to the reality inside the imagined scene. The cabaret scene reminds me of a Joseph von Sternberg movie with Marlene Dietrich as the slinky chanteuse. The "I" is titillated but

the images themselves are not titillating. Other people are objects, he is the tempted holy man.

> I sit at a gold table with my girl
> Whose eyelids burn with brandy. What a whirl
> Of Easter eggs is colored by the lights,
> As the Norwegian dancer's crystaled tights
> Flash with her naked leg's high-booted skate,
> Like Northern Lights upon my watching plate.
> The twinkling steel above me is a star;
> I am a fallen Christmas tree. . . .

Every word and phrase and image has an underside, spurred by
desire. The line, "I am a fallen Christmas tree," is a wicked jibe
at the family and everything he feels is constraining him from
having the kind of erotic experience he desires.

> I turn and whisper in her ear. You know
> I want to leave my mother and my wife,
> You wouldn't have me tied to them for life . . .

In these lines the lover and Katherine's father are merged; each
whispers in her ear and is unable to act. At this point we realize
that the narrator was Katherine's lover in the previous section
which, since this was not explicit, helps account for the secretive
quality of that passage.

The dichotomy between mind and body, and the psychological double bind in this poem are so intense that the narrator
literally disintegrates in the avalanche in the middle of the last
stanza.

> Time runs, the windshield runs with stars. The past
> Is cities from a train, until at last
> Its escalating and black-windowed blocks
> Recoil against a Gothic church. The clocks
> Are tolling. I am dying. The shocked stones
> Are falling like a ton of bricks and bones
> That snap and splinter and descend in glass
> Before a priest who mumbles through his Mass

For my own part I prefer this wild desperation and intensity to the cynicism and resignation in some of the later poems. Here Lowell is in a state of bleak ecstasy; there is a jolt when inner connections come, a prosodic shock. He writes as if everything were at stake, especially in the passage when he echoes Marlowe's *Faustus*.

> The starres moove stil, time runs, the clocke wil strike.
> The divel wil come, and Faustus must be damnd.
> O Ile leape up to my God: who pulles me downe?
> See, see where Christs blood streames in the firmament,
> One drop would save my soule, halfe a drop, ah my Christ.
> Ah rend not my heart for naming of my Christ,
> Yet wil I call on him: oh spare me *Lucifer!* [21]

These lines of Marlowe's are among the first examples of dramatic speech in blank verse, and some of the most powerful lines in the tradition. Lowell goes to the Elizabethans for energy and tension, and puts the influence to good use. The end of "Beyond the Porch and the Altar" replicates Faustus' farewell to the world.

> Here the Lord
> Is Lucifer in harness: hand on sword,
> He watches me for Mother, and will turn
> The bier and baby-carriage where I burn.
>
> (*SP* 19)

The narrator, like Faustus, wants to be spared, but first has to burn. You have to be damned, the poem argues, before you can be saved. He and Katherine are both cornered. At the poem's end Lowell introduces Lucifer, like a deus ex machina, to watch over the narrator in place of the mother, who is further transmogrified and gives her power over his death as well as his life.

Browning, Eliot, and Pound impersonate, in varying degrees, other voices; Lowell infuses the force of his own personality and style into every line he writes. The presence of this voice gives his oeuvre its overall unity; it enables him to assimilate a phenomenal variety of material into the fabric of his verse and into the persona he employed in his dramatic monologues.

This is why, when you read Lowell's work, any or all of it including the *imitations*/translations, you read Lowell. I don't think it a quirk on my part to think so. Some of the most realized poems in *Lord Weary's Castle* are the translations. In her review, Louise Bogan wrote,

> Lowell's technical competence is remarkable, and this book shows a definite advance over the rather stiff and crusty style of his first volume, *Land of Unlikeness*, published in 1944. This competence shows most clearly in his "imitations" and arrangements of the work of others, which he hesitates to call direct translations. "The Ghost" (after Sextus Propertius), "The Fens" (after Cobbett), and the poems derived from Valéry, Rimbaud, and Rilke reveal a new flexibility and directness.[22]

Imitations, like "The Ghost" (after Sextus Propertius), are the poetic equivalents of memento mori. "A ghost is someone: death has left a hole/ For the lead-colored soul to beat the fire." The presence of death here is so tangible, so present to the senses, that it fuels his imagination.

> Cynthia leaves her dirty pyre
> And seems to coil herself and roll
>   Under my canopy,
> Love's stale and public playground, where I lie
> And fill the run-down empire of my bed.
> I see the street, her potter's field, is red
> And lively with the ashes of the dead;

(*SP* 20)

Lowell got to Propertius through Pound's "Homage to Sextus Propertius," and when he read him in Latin found "a very excited, tense poet, rather desperate; his line is much more like parts of Marlowe's *Faustus*. And he's of all the Roman poets the most like a desperate Christian. His experiences, his love affair with Cynthia, are absolutely rending, destroying. He's like a fallen Christian" (*PRI* 356). Or, very much like Lowell in *Lord Weary's Castle*, obsessed by sex and death.

"Where the Rainbow Ends," the last poem in *Lord Weary's Castle*, begins:

> I saw the sky descending, black and white,
> Not blue, on Boston . . .
>
> (*SP* 33)

Lowell sets up a Manichean dualism in the first line and the construction "not blue" in the second line echoes the second line of the first poem in the book "The Exile's Return" with its "Not ice, not snow. . . ."

The three stanzas, using the same ten-line stanza he invented for "The Quaker Graveyard," can be viewed as triadic. In the first Lowell is a spectator, documenting the cold, barren Boston landscape "where winters wore/ The skulls to jack-o'-lanterns on the slates." In the second stanza he sees the Pepperpot bridge that spans the frozen river "and its scales of scorched-earth miles" transformed into "the Scales, the pans/ Of judgment rising and descending." His city, Boston, is being weighed in the balance. Lowell excoriates the people of this fallen world, tells them the day of doom has arrived. Like Jesus in the temple of the money-changers Lowell sees himself as a prophet, an instrument of God.

> And I am a red arrow on this graph
> Of Revelations. Every dove is sold

These lines had particular resonance for Lowell. They prompted Allen Ginsberg to dub him a "Beat Manqué" (LCR). And two of his closest and most trusted poet friends were sharply divided about them: Randall Jarrell told him to take them out; Delmore Schwartz told him to put them back in. He followed Schwartz's advice.

In the final stanza Lowell becomes an active agent in determining his own destiny, and undergoes an intense transforming experience through marriage. Lowell's attitude toward marriage is more geniunely religious, even if it is displaced (marriage is not religion), than it's been toward anything else. The symbolism remains: the grand mechanism winds down; he decides to say *no* to saying no.

> In Boston serpents whistle at the cold.
> The victim climbs the altar steps and sings:
> "Hosannah to the lion, lamb, and beast
> Who fans the furnace-face of IS with wings:
> I breathe the ether of my marriage feast."
> At the high altar, gold
> And a fair cloth. I kneel and the wings beat
> My cheek. What can the dove of Jesus give
> You now but wisdom, exile? Stand and live,
> The dove has brought an olive branch to eat.

Marriage resolves the initial dualism ("black and white/ Not blue") and the burden of the prophetic stance giving him access to freedom—a terrible freedom akin to Kierkegaard's possibility of possibility.

In later years Lowell came to have some sense of humor toward his early work. In a reading at the Library of Congress, October 31, 1960, he prefaced "Where the Rainbow Ends" with the following comments:

> It's an apocalyptic poem . . . it's the world coming to an end in Boston . . . (audience laughter). This was written during the war when . . . perhaps such thoughts come to one's mind rather easily . . . I pointed that out to an audience . . . said that I was a false prophet . . . that Boston was still there. In a question pe-

riod someone said, "Doesn't that make your poem weaker?" (audience laughter).

(LCR)

In "The Exile's Return" Lowell begins as an isolated walled-in being. Form was his fortress; but the man in the fortress can only look out. The last line of the poem, "*Voi ch'entrate*, and your life is in your hands," means he has to live his own life and to live he has to choose and to choose he has to fall and the fall is into time. He reveals throughout the book that no matter what he says about the condition of the modern world—it may be hell—there is more to life than passive acceptance of evil and he discovers responses to it other than excoriation.

Of all the poems in *Lord Weary's Castle*, "Where the Rainbow Ends," is one of the most decisive and final; tunneling through "the dead season" (*I* 8) like the worms who "eat the deadwood to the foot/ Of Ararat" (*SP* 33), burrowing backward in time to what William Carlos Williams in "The Descent" called "a sort of renewal" in marriage.[23] Marriage for Lowell is one solution to the condition of spiritual exile, prompting him to step down from his pedestal and become the "victim" who "climbs the altar steps," intoxicated by the ether of his marriage feast, and sings.

❧

From THE GREAT TESTAMENT
(*For William Carlos Williams*)

I am thirty this year,
near Christmas, the dead season,
when wolves live off the wind,
and the poor peasants fear
the icy firmament.
Sound in body and mind,

I write my Testament,
but the ink has frozen.

Where are those gallant men
I ran with in my youth?
They sang and spoke so well!
Ah nothing can survive
after the last amen;
some are perhaps in hell.
May they sleep in God's truth;
God save those still alive!

.   .   .

I think now of those skulls
piling up in the morgue—
all masters of the rolls,
or the king's treasurers,
or water-carriers,
or blacksmiths at the forge.
Who'll tell me which is which,
which poor, and which were rich?

.   .   .

Who cares then to die shriven?
Feet cramp, the nostrils curve,
eyes stare, the stretched veins hiss
and ache through joint and nerve—
Oh woman's body, poor,
supple, tender—is this
what you were waiting for?
Yes, or ascend to heaven.

(*I* 8, 11, 14; Villon: *Le grand testament*)

Lord Weary's Castle was published in Lowell's thirtieth year.

CHAPTER 2

An Interrupted Life

"You sit stiller" said Kokka
"if whenever you move something jangles."
—Ezra Pound

I am not one of them.
I was sent by God to torment
myself, my family, everyone
whom it's a sin to torment.

—Pasternak

Life Studies is the first major book of American poetry about the nuclear family. Previously this was the terrain of fiction and drama—of novels like Faulkner's *Absalom, Absalom* or O'Neill's *Long Day's Journey into Night*. Lowell breaks new ground for poetry. In the painful juncture between *The Mills of the Kavanaughs* and *Life Studies* he learned the possibilities inherent in a more transparent style—a style conceived as the revelation of a world, rather than an end in itself. Although the radical change in Lowell's poetry has often been described as a shift from the hieratic style of Allen Tate to the colloquial style of William Carlos Williams, Lowell's mature style, which emerges in *Life Studies*, reflects a synthesis of both potentialities.

Lowell's last reading in New York was with Allen Ginsberg at St. Mark's Church on the Bowery, Ginsberg's home turf.

Lowell was forthcoming and gracious that evening; he said; "Allen and I aren't as different as we're thought to be; we both come out of different aspects of Williams." Lowell wasn't saying anything he hadn't said before, but his emphasis on William Carlos Williams is tremendously significant. It's not even the influence of particular poems by Williams, but that Lowell was influenced by Williams' stance, and his attitude toward language and the world. He could write about his own bedroom. He could write about his own experiences in a sanatarium.

Life Studies is divided into four parts. The first three serve as a prologue to the fourth: Part One sets the historical, political, cultural context and framework for the poems; Part Two, "91 Revere Street," a long prose narrative, provides the family background which heightens the effect the later poems have on us; Part Three contains homages to four writers with whom Lowell identified. The family drama is enacted in Part Four, entitled "Life Studies." In this section he uses the actual details of his social and private life and explores the tabooed realm of feelings toward the family.

Life Studies has an intricate and complex structure. It is not merely a collection of interrelated poems written over a period of time, and the impact of reading it is more like reading *Absalom, Absalom*, with its interconnected destinies, than a book of poems. The very first poem in Part One, "Beyond the Alps," exposes three of Lowell's recurrent themes: the disintegration of culture ("Now Paris, our black classic, breaking up/ like killer kings on an Etruscan cup"); his change in focus from the religious to the historical (the major change in culture over the last two hundred years); and his fascination with men of power.

> Much against my will
> I left the City of God where it belongs.
> There the skirt-mad Mussolini unfurled

the eagle of Caesar. He was one of us
only, pure prose. . . .

(SP 55)

"Beyond the Alps" has a playful grandeur, an *opera buffa* humor.
The archness of the earlier books is gone. Lowell has entered
the fallen world. He has found a form that is intimate and immediate and that does not sacrifice intensity for intimacy.

"Inauguration Day, January 1953" reminds us that these
poems were written during the Eisenhower era, the beginning
of the Cold War, "the tranquillized *Fifties*," as Lowell dubbed
them in "Memories of West Street and Lepke."

> Ice, ice. Our wheels no longer move.
> Look, the fixed stars, all just alike
> as lack-land atoms, split apart,
> and the Republic summons Ike,
> the mausoleum in her heart.

("Inauguration Day: January 1953," SP 57)

This kind of perception, in which the poetry interesects with
the historical moment ("alike"/"Ike") made Lowell "relevant."
Lowell's project in *Life Studies* can be regarded as a corrective to
conformity and the pernicious apathy he saw everywhere.

Part Three, with its portraits of Ford Madox Ford, George
Santayana, Hart Crane, and Delmore Schwartz, serves as an
invocation—a kind of entrance—to the "Life Studies" section of
Life Studies. It is the spiritual condition of exile that allies them
to Lowell. These men stand in marked contrast to the characters
in the "Life Studies" section. The theme of these homages is
redemption through writing well, the hazards of the profession,
and the strange comforts afforded by it.

In "Ford Madox Ford" Lowell relishes the mischievous an-
tics of Ford, who broke one of the cardinal rules of golf—suc-

cessfully, no less—causing Lloyd George to have an apoplectic
fit.

> The lobbed ball plops, then dribbles to the cup . . . .
> (a birdie Fordie!) But it nearly killed
> the ministers. Lloyd George was holding up
> the flag. He gabbled, "Hop-toad, hop-toad, hop-toad!
> Hueffer has used a niblick on the green;
> it's filthy art, Sir, filthy art!"
> You answered, "What is art to me and thee?
> Will a blacksmith teach a midwife how to bear?"
> That cut the puffing statesman down to size,
> Ford. You said, "Otherwise,
> I would have been general of a division." . . .
>
> (*SP* 59)

The poem opens with the ball in the air—a momentarily
suspended action. The slow, rising tongue-twisting sounds of
the beginning parallel the arc of the "lobbed ball" which heads
toward the cup the moment it "plops." This motion sets the
poem into motion. The difference in the pacing of each line not
only matches the action but also duplicates the tension and release of the players waiting for the ball to stop, as though they
had been holding their breath until the ball drops.

The poem has an elastic texture. In three linked and son-
netlike sections (the rhyme scheme in the last fourteen lines is
abab, cddc, efg, fge) Lowell creates a hybrid lyric form that
allows him to incorporate dramatic dialogue, narrative, flash-
back, recitative. It is remarkable how much of Ford's life he gets
into forty-five lines (through his "art").

Lloyd George goads Ford: "It's filthy art, Sir." Ford "scores"
off him again with his retort, "What is art to me and thee?" But
it is only a momentary victory—it contains the essence of Ford's
attitude towards authority, an attitude that may have served him
for his art but which defeated him in life. "Ford Madox Ford's
friends used to excuse Ford by saying he would condescend to

God if given the opportunity."[1] Not everyone was as inclined to forgive him.

The rest of the poem tracks Ford through a disastrous military career, bad marriages and affairs—Ford was perpetually in trouble with women:

> a Jonah—O divorced, divorced
> from the whale-fat of post-war London! Boomed,
> cut, plucked and booted! In Provence, New York . . .
> marrying, blowing . . . nearly dying

Lowell telescopes Ford's life through a series of transformations: from "blowing" whalelike, "nearly dying/ at Boulder, when the altitude/ pressed the world on your heart"; to floundering like a fish gasping for air out of water "with fish-blue-eyes,/ and mouth pushed out/ fish-fashion"; and then, with no compunction about mixing metaphors, "Wheel-horse, O unforgetting elephant." No one term is mammoth enough to encompass Ford's Falstaffian presence.

> But master, mammoth mumbler, tell me why
> the bales of your left-over novels buy
> less than a bandage for your gouty foot.

In the last lines of the poem, Lowell apologizes to Ford for selling him short, for dealing with his lived life when it was his "lies," the life of his imagination, his "Fiction!" that made "the great [his] equals." This apology makes way for the heartbreaking, quiet, and compassionate last line.

> Fiction! I'm selling short
> your lies that made the great your equals. Ford,
> you were a kind man and you died in want.

"Selling short" anticipates Lowell's portrait of his father, Commander Lowell, who worked for a time as an "investment advisor." The stock market terms and the golf games tie the poems together. It's Ford's genuine incompetence that interests Lowell—and the fact that, in a pathetic way, he was "a kind man." Lowell loves him for his incompetence.

※∜≮

For a poet who was so scarred by self-laceration, who lashed himself mercilessly for transgressions that remain nameless, "examining and then examining/ what I really have against myself" ("Symptoms," *SP* 228), he was uncommonly generous to his friends in his renditions of them, faithful to the most fatal detail. He gave others a tenderness he denied himself, as though friendship represented an escape from the strife of love.

Lowell learned how to do this from novelists rather than poets—especially Tolstoy, whom Lowell acknowledged as a conscious model:

> The ideal modern form seems to be the novel and certain short stories. Maybe Tolstoy would be the perfect example—his work is imagistic, it deals with all experience, and there seems to be no conflict of the form and content. So one thing is to get into poetry that kind of human richness in simple descriptive language.
>
> *(PRI* 343)

This is an extraordinary way for a poet to talk. Lowell doesn't separate his thoughts about poetry from his thoughts about prose; he sees them as allies, conjoint operations, joined by elective affinities. In back of this is Pound's injunction that "poetry has to be as well written as prose," an extraordinary challenge to an art that by the end of the century had become sloppy, overly refined, given over to pure verbal music, and lacked true tension between words and things; and in back of Pound's injunction is the model of Flaubert's prose, and the unthought-of possibilities it could open up for poetry.

When Lowell refers to prose, his emphasis is on *content*—the signs and characteristic unconscious gestures through which people reveal themselves. Tolstoy's mastery is indicated by the extent to which he can suggest the totality of a character through details and gestures: in *Anna Karenina* there's Karenin's habit of cracking his knuckles—the only sign he shows of being out of control—nasty but human; and Vronsky's encroaching baldness that undermines his dashing exterior and, insofar as his self-image is bound up with his good looks, parallels his diminishing sense of his own power. To make this concrete, consider what Tolstoy is able to reveal in one paragraph of *War and Peace* about an unnamed, completely minor character, through a plethora of adjectives and active verbs:

> The regimental commander was a sanguine, thickset, middle-aged general with grizzled eyebrows and whiskers, broader from chest to back than across the shoulders. He wore a brand-new uniform, still creased where it had been folded, and thick gold epaulettes that seemed to stand up rather than lie on his corpulent shoulders. As he walked up and down in front of the line, his back slightly arched, his body quivering at every step, he had the air of a man happily performing one of life's most sacred duties. It was not hard to see that the commander admired his regiment, delighted in it, and that his mind was completely taken up with it; yet for all this, his quivering strut seemed to suggest that, over and above his military interests, social life and the fair sex occupied a considerable place in his thoughts.[2]

As always in Tolstoy, it is a cutting down to life size; and the figure is somewhat antiheroic and a little absurd. We know (without knowing it) that such unblemished enthusiasm and vigor will allow the regiment, and by extension the whole Russian army, to defeat the heretofore invincible Napoleon. Lowell's recognition that this kind of prose could open up a new terrain for poetry is evident from the first stanza of *Life Studies*. He put forth his new aesthetic credo in a wryly humorous aside on "the skirt-mad Mussolini": "He was one of us/ only, pure prose" ("Beyond the Alps").

The poems in Part Four, "Life Studies," consolidated Lowell's reputation. In his essay "The Age of Lowell," published in 1965, Irvin Ehrenpreis stated: "It is not easy to overpraise *Life Studies*."[3] One of the striking things about that comment is not its content so much as the time it was written. At the age of forty-eight Lowell was living dangerously in "The Age of Lowell," and from then on he was always under pressure to live up to the bubble of this reputation, which added to his sense of burden and the difficulty he had in living.

In his previous books, the length and structure of his poems seemed too predetermined, even overdetermined, which means to me that there's a lot he *had* to leave out and a lot he *had* to put in, when neither "had" was always integral to the meaning of the poem. Once he gets "Beyond the Alps," and through the screens of friends, he can return home, in imagination, without qualms; from this point on the language does not often dominate the poems.

What emerges in Part Four is another Robert Lowell, or Robert Lowell as another, who bears as much relationship to the real Robert Lowell as the real Walt Whitman did to the Walt Whitman embodied in *Leaves of Grass*. The freedom involved here has to do entirely with art, the exigencies that are imposed upon an artist by his medium. Lowell does more than project his own personality; he creates the personality that he projects.

In "Life Studies" we are thrust into the action immediately; the narrator, this time, is the real imagined Robert Lowell, whose history corresponds, rather than conforms, to the "I" in the poems. Lowell is *in* the poems.

"I won't go with you. I want to stay with Grandpa!"
That's how I threw cold water
on my Mother and Father's
watery martini pipe dreams at Sunday dinner.
("My Last Afternoon with Uncle Devereux Winslow," I, *SP* 66)

In "Life Studies" Lowell thrusts his imagination back in
time and gets the closed capsule of his past to open—redolent
with life! Caught between generations, he didn't have access to
the sort of fresh experience, the freedom, or for that matter the
spontaneity that, say, Gary Snyder has in a poem like "Bubbs
Creek Haircut," which begins in the present with Snyder getting a haircut before hitching a ride into the mountains:

High ceilingd and the double mirrors, the
        calendar a splendid alpine scene—scab barber—
in stained white barber gown, alone, sat down, old man
A summer fog gray San Francisco day
I walked right in. on Howard Street
                    haircut a dollar twenty-five.
Just clip it close as it will go.
        "now why you want your hair cut back like that."
        —well I'm going to the Sierras for a while
Bubbs Creek and on across to upper Kern.
                    he wriggled clippers,
"Well I been up there, I built the cabin
        up at Cedar Grove. In nineteen five."
                    old haircut smell . . .[4]

Snyder, for whom poetry is "a riprap on the slick rock of metaphysics,"[5] wants his poems to register pleasure. He feels his
freedom keenly: desires life without luggage—and relies on his
senses, intuition, and intelligence to tell him what he needs.

Lowell claims that hearing "the beats" read in San Francisco, where he was on a reading tour, helped inspire his second
birth as a poet. Here were young, gifted, vital poets writing
directly about their lives as lived, while he, Lowell, was writing
dramatic monologues in clotted end-stopped iambic pentameter

couplets. Lowell learns how to begin a poem in the present but first he has to touch ground in his childhood or someplace in the past before he can go on. He is able to assimilate the formal impulse—the very idea of beginning at the beginning, but the same things that provoke Snyder to go forward in time propel Lowell backward. It is in the wonder and awe and bewilderment and terror of the child's perception that his still lifes come to life.

"Life Studies" begins with the most unclouded eye in the book—the child's eye in poems like "My Last Afternoon with Uncle Devereux Winslow," "Dunbarton," and "Commander Lowell." We know that children see a proportionally different world from adults—small things look big to them and they haven't become chained to habit. "What were those sunflowers? Pumpkins floating shoulder-high?" (*SP* 67). One reason Rimbaud thought, to be completely modern, poetry had to begin with the systematic derangement of the senses, is that adults around him had been numbed by habit and he could see that they no longer saw. Habit dulls us and obliterates our capacity to make choices, to act. Yet it is also a survival mechanism: it cuts down the pain of living.

In these poems about his childhood, Lowell consciously stays on the surface to present his perceptions clearly:

> Our farmer was cementing a root-house under the hill.
> One of my hands was cool on a pile
> of black earth, the other warm
> on a pile of lime. All about me
> were the works of my Grandfather's hands:
>
> ("My Last Afternoon with Uncle
> Devereux Winslow," *SP* 66–67)

By following the trail of the details, by being attentive to the subtle signs of disturbance (the child doesn't know what he's feeling), Lowell renders the unconscious gestures that convey his pain.

> No one had died there in my lifetime . . .
> Only Cinder, our Scottie puppy
> paralyzed from gobbling toads.
> I sat mixing black earth and lime.

These lines are cut true and they cleave to the rhythm they create. The whole poem is scaled to the child's perceptions. What he unearths is painful and unassimilable to the five-year-old "I," who feels something is amiss and ends up miming his confusion with his hands.

The connection between the perceptions is not at all forced and the recognition of mortality at the end has evolved—literally—out of substance—"earth and lime." Lowell has followed the trail of his own imagination through his perception of these details and his attention to these subtle and unconscious signs of anxiety and terror in the child.

I said earlier that the book has a complex and intricate structure. The poems are held together through recurrent themes—the breakdown of the old social order, represented by Grandfather Winslow, and the dissolution of the nuclear family; the recurrent use of animal imagery—whales, horses, seals—not in any allegorical sense but for their physical and psychological connotations; and recurrent symbols of masculine prowess such as canes:

> I borrowed Grandfather's cane
> carved with the names and altitudes
> of Norwegian mountains he had scaled—
> *more a weapon than a crutch*
> > > ("Dunbarton," *SP* 73, italics mine)

as well as swords ("I nagged for his dress sword with gold braid" ["Commander Lowell"]), golf courses, and especially cars:

My parents' confidences and quarrels stopped each night at ten or eleven o'clock, when my father would hang up his tuxedo, put on his commander's uniform, and take a trolley back to the naval yard at Charlestown. He had just broken in a new car. Like a chauffeur, he watched this car, a Hudson, with an informed vigilance, always giving its engine hair-trigger little tinkerings of adjustment or friendship, always fearful lest the black body, unbeautiful as his boiled shirts, should lose its outline and gloss. He drove with flawless, almost instrumental, monotony.

("91 Revere Street," *LS* 22–23)

On our yearly autumn get-aways from Boston
to the family graveyard in Dunbarton,
he took the wheel himself—
like an admiral at the helm.
Freed from Karl and chuckling over the gas he was saving,
he let his motor roller-coaster
out of control down each hill.

("Dunbarton," *SP* 72)

They're altogether otherworldly now,
those adults champing for their ritual Friday spin
to pharmacist and five-and-ten in Brockton.

.   .   .

the Pierce Arrow clears its throat in a horse stall.

("Grandparents," *SP* 74)

He was soon fired. Year after year,
he still hummed "Anchors aweigh" in the tub—
whenever he left a job,
he bought a smarter car.

("Commander Lowell," *SP* 77)

The local dealer, a "buccaneer,"
had been bribed a "king's ransom"
to quickly deliver a car without chrome.

("Terminal Days at Beverly Farms," *SP* 79)

my Tudor Ford climbed the hill's skull;
I watched for love-cars.

("Skunk Hour," *SP* 95–96)

Reading through the poems, the repetition gives the impression of mirrors set up to reflect one another, each shedding new light and meaning on the other. This mirroring is integral to the inner structure of *Life Studies* and helps turn it from a collection of poems into a book. The mirror's potentially distorting effect is what gives *Life Studies* its eerie quality.

> Distorting drops of water
> pinpricked my face in the basin's mirror.
> I was a stuffed toucan
> with a bibulous, multicolored beak.
>
> ("My Last Afternoon with Uncle
> Devereux Winslow, *SP* 68)

Everything connects in this air of lost connections: Ford Madox Ford and Commander Lowell, Czar Lepke (head of Murder, Inc.) and Robert Lowell. Through this process the poet comes to see all these possibilities within himself.

Life Studies is a book about violence, fragmentation, "lost connections," the disruption of order, about *breaking*. In this sense it is a microcosmic portrait of American society in a time of crisis.

❧

"Commander Lowell" is a chilling portrayal of Lowell's immediate family. Although ostensibly about the father, it is really a triple portrait: of mother, of father, of son. The poem begins with the poet's recollection of his early childhood when his father, a Naval officer, was away from home.

In a few lines, Lowell traces his father's decline after he succumbs to his wife's demands to resign his commission ("With seamanlike celerity,/ Father left the Navy,/ and deeded Mother his property") and drifts from one job to another from his first position, a well-paying job at Lever Brothers, to his last at "Scudder, Stevens and Clark, Investment Advisors,/ himself his only client." Lowell's description of his father in "91 Revere Street" is pathetic, if not heartbreaking: "Father resigned from the service in 1927, but he never had a civilian *career*; he instead had merely twenty-two years of the civilian *life*" (*LS* 15).

In the poem Lowell gives us a stereoscopic view of his father's "civilian life." Unlike Ford Madox Ford, he was the object of ridicule on the golf course at "the summer colony at 'Matt' " when he

> took four shots with his putter to sink his putt.
> "Bob," they said, "golf's a game you really ought to know how to play, if you play at all."
> They wrote him off as "naval,"
> naturally supposed his sport was sailing.
>
> (*SP* 76–77)

Lowell's father, unlike Ford, does *not* come up with a punch line. It's given to the men who are contemptuous of him, while he's written off as "naval." But he was never accepted by the "seadogs" at the yacht club either. ("Poor Father, his training was engineering!") and he was "lost/ in the mob of ruling-class Bostonians."

In "Commander Lowell" the poet reveals the source of some of his primal conflicts. His father's long absences left him alone with his mother who pumped him full of her frustrated ambitions, filled him with her unappeased longing ("Her voice was still electric/ with a hysterical, unmarried panic") and fueled his fantasy life with images of generals ("I . . . got two hundred French generals by name,/ from *A* to *V*—from Augereau to Vandamme"). She makes him feel embarrassed that his father is a Naval officer.

It was a claustrophobic atmosphere for the child to grow up in. "There were no undesirables or girls in my set,/ when I was a boy at Mattapoisett—/ only Mother, still her Father's daughter." In the poem we see the father in the light of this mother-son conspiracy. One wonders why Lowell's parents didn't get divorced given this loveless marriage, except to prolong the mutual torment.

> While Mother dragged to bed alone,
> read Menninger,
> and grew more and more suspicious,
> he grew defiant.

The relationship depicted in the poem between his parents resembles that of Charles and Emma Bovary, evidenced in the point of view of the mother toward the father, and in the way Emma and his mother use reading as substitutes for passion. There's some grim humor in this passage: Emma Bovary reads novels that fuel her romantic imagination and bring out her contempt for her unambitious husband; Lowell's mother turns to psychology, which increases her suspicion that her depressed husband has lost contact with reality and which gives her ammunition that contributes to the man's ongoing emasculation.

Throughout the poem the father is described as a man who wasn't "serious," his outward exterior was "cheerful and cowed," he continued "smiling on all" even after squandering sixty thousand dollars in three years with his "piker speculations."

But the portrait is more one of a man who retreated into a life of fantasy.

> Night after night,
> *à la clarté déserte de sa lampe,*
> he slid his ivory Annapolis slide rule
> across a pad of graphs—
> piker speculations! . . .

His "ivory Annapolis slide rule" has replaced his "dress sword with gold braid," as a symbol of his manhood. This passage, which brings the father to center stage through the lulling repetition of "night," the French quotation, and his treasured slide rule, shows his father at his lowest—at his most deluded. It is one thing for the child to dream or dope himself to sleep memorizing the names of generals. But Lowell's father has become a child, allowing himself to be unmanned by his castrating wife. The child's reverie turns to dust in the adult's mouth.

> Pour l'enfant, amoureux de cartes et d'estampes,
> L'univers est égal à son vaste appétit.
> *Ah! que le monde est grand à la clarté des lampes!*
> Aux yeux du souvenir que le monde est petit![6]
> ("Le Voyage," Baudelaire; italics mine)

In *Imitations* Lowell translated these lines of Baudelaire, further illuminating the tone of his father's lamplit excursions to nowhere.

> For the boy playing with his globe and stamps,
> the world is equal to his appetite—
> how grand the world in the blaze of the lamps,
> how petty in tomorrow's small dry light!
> ("The Voyage," *I* 66; Baudelaire: *Le voyage*)

Nonetheless, returning to "Commander Lowell," we register that a subtle shift in tone has occurred. From here on the poet retains the irony but retracts the contempt. It is as if the poem had been written from different stages in the development of Lowell's consciousness. The older poet, now himself a man in his forties, can feel some compassion and the end of the poem is an attempt to redeem his father who "as early as 1928" had the foresight to own "a house converted to oil," which had a drawing room " 'longitudinal as Versailles.' "

> And once
> nineteen, the youngest ensign in his class,
> he was "the old man" of a gunboat on the Yangtze.

Young Lowell has some of the toughness and resilience of the boy in Rimbaud's poem, "The Poet at Seven," which Lowell later adapts in *Imitations*. There are several similarities between the two poems: structure and form; the look of the poem on the page; the role of the mother—who reads to her son and creates a smothering atmosphere, a prison from which the boy longs to escape.

> All day he would sweat obedience.
>
> . . .
>
> His worst block,
> was the stultifying slump
> of mid-summer—he would lock
> himself up in the toilet and inhale
> its freshness; there he could breathe.
>
> . . .
>
> At seven he was making novels
> about life in the Sahara,
> where ravished Liberty had fled—
> sunrises, buffaloes, jungle, savannahs!
> For his facts, he used illustrated weeklies,
> and blushed at the rotogravures of naked, red
> Hawaiian girls dancing.
>
> ("The Poet at Seven," *I* 77–78;
> Rimbaud: *Les poètes de sept ans*)

What figures most prominently in "Commander Lowell" and "The Poet at Seven" is that both children discover an escape from the claustrophia of the mother's tyranny and seek satisfaction in imagination, in language.

Roland Barthes asks

> How can one have an erotic relationship with proper names? No suspicion of metonymy. . . . And yet, [it's] impossible to read a novel, or memoirs without that special greediness. . . . It is not merely a linguistics of proper names which is needed but an erotics as well: names, like voices, like odors, would be the terms of a languor: desire and death: "The last sigh which remains of things," says an author of the last century.[7]

Reading this passage made me return to the opening lines of "Commander Lowell."

> There were no undesirables or girls in my set,
> when I was a boy at Mattapoisett—

Imagine getting a word like "Mattapoisett" into a poem! Not only does the sound delight but it rhymes with "set" *and* it reminds us of "Madaket" in "The Quaker Graveyard in Nantucket." After the dash anything can happen—but what does it lead him to this time? Not the sea "still breaking violently" but "only Mother, still her Father's daughter." This is an essential detail rendered without unnatural stress, and an instance of Lowell's mastery of the techniques of narrative prose. So is the way he undercuts the father, who has sabotaged his own interests, by using the phrase "seamanlike celerity," with its blatant sexual overtones, to describe how his father "deeded Mother his property," handing over his power in this gesture. The sting is compounded because the Commander was not a sailor of any kind, but an engineer. We know from "91 Revere Street" that the real Commander was "Father's old Annapolis roommate, Commander Billy 'Battleship Bilge' Harkness" (p. 32), that Billy replaced his father in Robert's memory, and became the model for the powerful men who figure so prominently in his work, from Napoleon to "Attila/Hitler."

> The man who seems in my memory to sit under old Mordecai's portrait is not my father, but Commander Billy—*the* Commander after Father had thrown in his commission. There Billy would sit glowing, perspiring, bragging. Despite his rowdiness, he even then *breathed the power* that would make him a vice-admiral and hero in World War II.
>
> ("91 Revere Street," *LS* 45)

In "Commander Lowell," the poet drills in the sadness and pathos of his father's last job, where he was out of his element, playing the market—another game he didn't know—ending up with "himself his only client," through the enunciation of these syllables: "Scudder, Stevens and Clark, Investment Advisors." The name of the firm itself, the coldness and impersonality, rises up suddenly like a gigantic monolith to dwarf the beached Commander.

"Commander Lowell" further demonstrates the telescopic power of Lowell's poetic imagination. He manages to convey the essence of "91 Revere Street," which is thirty-five pages long, in a poem of seventy-three lines and gives us a coherent psychological framework within which to consider the detotalized totality of his vast life's work.

※※

After the family portraits in the early part of the "Life Studies" section, Lowell's imagination explodes and he writes four major poems: "Waking in the Blue," "Memories of West Street and Lepke," "Man and Wife," and "Skunk Hour." From this point on it is as if his nuclear family had dissolved; he begins to treat the world as an extended family. One of Lowell's defining characteristics as a poet is worldliness: his familiarity with people from all walks of life and all times of history. The price of his insights is madness. In the beginning of "Waking in the Blue," we find him at McLean's, "the house for the 'mentally ill' "; in "Memories of West Street and Lepke" he's in jail. His descents into the underworld enable him to see the world around him with heightened clarity, give him a sense of hyperreality.

Even when Lowell writes about extreme situations of terrible mental stress, the seeing eye is fantastically lucid. His mimicry of a natural voice is matchless. He makes us think that we're being let in on some ongoing dialogue: half directed outward, half inward—just clear enough and just vague enough to engage us. He carves his art out of a deep sense of unease.

"Waking in the Blue" begins:

> The night attendant, a B.U. sophomore,
> rouses from the mare's-nest of his drowsy head
> propped on *The Meaning of Meaning.*
> He catwalks down our corridor.

(SP 87)

Alas, Lowell is embarrassed to tell us where he is, and so starts a diversionary tactic, fixing on the most outwardly normal character, the one figure in the poem who is not deranged, an earlier version of Lowell perhaps who, unlike the "night attendant," stayed awake reading *The Meaning of Meaning.* The night attendant has a sinister sanity; in this context his is a terrible innocence. There's a hint of danger as well as caution in the way he moves silently down the corridor—as if these dark nights of the soul could be attended to.

> Azure day
> makes my agonized blue window bleaker.
> Crows maunder on the petrified fairway.

"Azure day" has the same doubleness as the "night attendant": "azure" is too romantic for Lowell's sensibility; he is not an azure poet. So he turns the word against itself. The brightness upsets him. The landscape becomes bleaker in the blinding light and what once lived is now dead. "Crows maunder on the petrified fairway." In this line, as in certain expressionist paintings, the subject moves through the object that has already permeated the subject. The line operates aptly at many levels. The dramatic situation curbs his rhetoric and allows him to put his resources to work. The strong verb "maunder" propels the action forward and the adjective "petrified" embraces the noun.

These words—"maunder" and "petrified"—express Lowell's own depression and terror. It is possible to subtract them from the line and still have an image—one that resembles a literal translation of a haiku—of crows on a fairway (which is neutral enough, if bleak); but the controlling image in Lowell's line has less to do with crows and fairways than what it feels like to "maunder" and be "petrified." He stops time and the winter fairway links necessarily to the frozen mind.

The deserted golf course and the maundering crows remind him of his own isolation, piercing him to the bone, and he cries out—

> Absence! My heart grows tense
> as though a harpoon were sparring for the kill.

And only now makes explicit reference, in subtones, in a kind of aside to where he is,

> (This is the house for the "mentally ill.")

Looking around the ward, Lowell finds he has no one to talk to: Stanley, "a kingly granite profile in a crimson golf cap," is "more cut off from words than a seal"; Bobbie, "redolent and roly-poly as a sperm whale," "swashbuckles about in his birthday suit." These mad figures, pushed out of the stream of life into fantasy, have been reduced to animality in the madhouse. Since their minds are gone, the only way Lowell can define them is through their bodies.

> These victorious figures of bravado ossified young.

This is one of the lines that when I first read Lowell made me do a doubletake—paradox links to paradox: "victorious"/ "bravado" and "ossified"/"young." In one line through this condensed language, Lowell integrates the many sides of otherwise unresolvable issues, arguments, and situations. It brings to mind one of Lowell's most cryptic and useful insights as recorded by Frank Bidart: "You can say anything in a poem—if you *place* it properly."

Lowell finds relief from his desperation through his observations. Stanley and Bobbie are both Harvard men, symbolically ruined kings, the former "now sunk in his sixties," was "once a Harvard all-American fullback/ (if such were possible!)," the latter "a replica of Louis XVI/ without the wig." He sets up another set of contrasts between these shipwrecks of Yankee culture, the "Mayflower/screwballs" like Lowell, himself, and the humorless "slightly too little nonsensical . . . Roman Catholic attendants."

The meaning of the poem hinges on the twist in the last stanza. Up to this point he's focused our attention on others. He gives us the illusion of health and buoyant confidence, beginning with "a hearty New England breakfast." This rodomontade makes the conclusion all the more rending. He hints of what is to come when he describes himself in animal terms:

> Cock of the walk,
> I strut in my turtle-necked French sailor's jersey
> before the metal shaving mirrors,
> and see the shaky figure grow familiar
> in the pinched, indigenous faces
> of these thoroughbred mental cases,
> twice my age and half my weight.
> We are all old-timers,
> each of us holds a locked razor.

The "locked razor" symbolizes the violence they would direct against themselves or others if they had the chance. The "metal shaving mirrors," there to prevent the inmates from hurting themselves with broken glass, distort the reflection, making the "future" shaky.

Lowell's lack of neutrality towards his subjects gives his

poems the very inwardness they need. In his best work, people, objects, and landscapes correspond precisely to interior states of mind. In this poem, the poet has been fighting the reality of his circumstance, which accounts for the poetic beginning with its "azure day" and the more literary language of "My heart grows tense/ as though a harpoon were sparring for the kill" with its echoes of *Moby Dick* and Lowell's own "Quaker Graveyard" and its foreshadowing of seal-like Stanley and whale-shaped Bobbie. It is as if this whole poem had taken place before the irregular surface of a metal mirror. And only at the end does he come to the terrible recognition that the other characters in the poem see him as one of them, that he, the observer, is one of the observed.

Heidegger insists that "being" is on its way, that wandering and poetry are allied. It is striking that in many of Lowell's best poems, the narrator is in motion—walking, on his feet. In these poems less attention is drawn to the language itself; the poet is not the passive victim of his own dread bolted imagination. Once he begins to move, the rhythm of the language is closer to the rhythm of the human gait. It is still highly wrought, but has an additional dimension which is understated—and the realm of *feeling* expands tremendously: "Strolling,/ I yammered metaphysics with Abramowitz" (*SP* 91). Lowell creates the contexts in which to act, and in which his language could become more active by virtue of circumstance, location, dramatic situation.

In "Memories of West Street and Lepke," Lowell recalls the time he spent in the West Street Jail in New York City during World War II.

> I was a fire-breathing Catholic C.O.,
> and made my manic statement,
> telling off the state and president, . . .

(SP 91)

The occasion further enlarged his extended family and range of connections. The jail is filled with antithetical types: it is there that he meets Abramowitz, a "fly-weight pacifist,/ so vegetarian,/ he wore rope shoes and preferred fallen fruit"; "Bioff and Brown,/ the Hollywood pimps . . . Hairy, muscular, suburban"; the Jehovah's Witness who taught him "the 'hospital tuck,'/ and pointed out the T-shirted back/ of *Murder Incorporated*'s Czar Lepke."

The poem has a triadic structure: It begins in the present tense with the poet "book-worming/ in pajamas fresh from the washer each morning," hogging "a whole house on Boston's/ 'hardly passionate Marlborough Street.' " The situation provokes a memory and the poem expands back in time, leading us naturally and unhurriedly to Czar Lepke. Only then does Lowell zoom in on his subject and through close attention to a series of details peculiar to Lepke begins to draw the parallels that unite him in his own mind to Lepke: Lepke was at home, so to speak, wearing a T-shirt, "piling towels on a rack," and Lowell is wearing pajamas "fresh from the washer"; Lepke was a privileged inmate and lives in a "segregated cell full/ of things forbidden the common man," and Lowell lives a privileged life on " 'hardly passionate Marlborough Street' " and has just returned from McLean's where he received shock treatment, and both his mania *and* his inspiration have fled: "Cured, I am frizzled, stale and small" ("Home After Three Months Away," *SP* 90). Lepke was:

> Flabby, bald, lobotomized,
> he drifted in a sheepish calm,
> where no agonizing reappraisal
> jarred his concentration on the electric chair—
> hanging like an oasis in his air
> of lost connections. . . .

Even at the end of the poem we are unprepared for this final comparison. We know that this is not a literal parallel;

Lowell, as a "fire-breathing Catholic C.O." was outwardly Lepke's opposite. Lepke doesn't strut or stroll, he dawdles; his possessions are a travesty of patriotism and religion considering who he is. Witness the "two toy American/ flags tied together with a ribbon of Easter palm" on his dresser. But what draws Lowell to Lepke in a deeper sense than the ironic details would suggest is his obsession with power, and at the time the poem was written, Lowell, just home from McLean's, felt he, too, was living in an "air/ of lost connections."

"Memories of West Street and Lepke" prefigures Lowell's later treatment of historical figures, the individualized portraits which fill the pages of *History*, portraits that are always partial self-portraits. Compare his treatment of Lepke with that of Cicero:

> Cicero bold, garrulous in his den
> chatting as host on his sofa of magazines;
> a squad of state doctors stands by him winking . . .
> he minds his hands shaking, and they keep shaking;
> if infirmity has a color, it isn't yellow.
> ("Cicero, the Sacrificial Killing," *SP* 162)

or, more tragically and incisively, with Coleridge:

> his passive courage is paralysis,
> standing him upright like tenpins for the strike,
> only kept standing by a hundred scared habits . . .
> a large soft-textured plant with pith within,
> power without strength, an involuntary imposter.
> ("Coleridge," *SP* 174)

"Memories of West Street and Lepke" bears a strong resemblance to "Waking in the Blue"—metaphorically, because of the confinement, and structurally, because of the insights revealed at the end of the poems that link Lowell to the others. With these two poems the poet intends us to ask ourselves who are

the mad people, who are the criminals; but he gives us two un-
tenable alternatives to existence—one is retreat into fantasy, the
other is violence to self or others. This was Lowell's emotional
dilemma—his vacillation between pacifism and violence. Looking back we remember Delmore Schwartz and Hart Crane, who
turned their violence inward, and Commander Lowell, Bobbie,
and Stanley, who retreated into fantasy. Looking ahead we find
Lowell exhausted in "Skunk Hour" by this quandary.

❧

"Man and Wife" takes place in the narrowest circle beyond
the self. The poem benefits from being addressed to a definite
other, a "you" who tempers the self's inclination to rhetorical
flourishes through its resistance. The presence of the addressee
in the poem gives it a focus, a center, a magnetic core that draws
him back into the past and makes it possible for him to remi-
nisce about what, for them, was an essential moment.

There isn't a wasted word in "Man and Wife" and the re-
currence of poetic devices (sound patterns, rhythms, and cadences) from earlier poems adds to its power. Nowhere are
Lowell's own ideas about the lyric better realized than here.

> The lyric, he said, quoting Keats's remark about "one eternal
> pant," is "a monument to immediacy". . . . A poem "*is* an event,
> not a record of an event." "It makes a claim to produce an event—
> it is this for which lyric strives and which it sometimes brings
> off." Lowell instanced "Keats's most fascinating poem," "This
> living hand," as a case in point in which, as Keats "eschews apos-
> trophe for direct address," he produces an event.[8]

We move from Lowell's portrait of Lepke to "Man and Wife"
where magnolias in blossom are murderous and the poet has

been saved for the fourth time by his wife, who has brought
him back from "the kingdom of the mad."

MAN AND WIFE

Tamed by *Miltown*, we lie on Mother's bed;
the rising sun in war paint dyes us red;
in broad daylight her gilded bed-posts shine,
abandoned, almost Dionysian.
At last the trees are green on Marlborough Street,
blossoms on our magnolia ignite
the morning with their murderous five days' white.
All night I've held your hand,
as if you had
a fourth time faced the kingdom of the mad—
its hackneyed speech, its homicidal eye—
and dragged me home alive. . . . Oh my *Petite*,
clearest of all God's creatures, still all air and nerve:
you were in your twenties, and I,
once hand on glass
and heart in mouth,
outdrank the Rahvs in the heat
of Greenwich Village, fainting at your feet—
too boiled and shy
and poker-faced to make a pass,
while the shrill verve
of your invective scorched the traditional South.

Now twelve years later, you turn your back.
Sleepless, you hold
your pillow to your hollows like a child;
your old-fashioned tirade—
loving, rapid, merciless—
breaks like the Atlantic Ocean on my head.

(*SP* 93)

I have a hunch that Miltown, in addition to being the drug of
the "tranquilized *Fifties*," is an intended pun on Milton, Lowell's

old master and possible spectre. Certainly the third and fourth lines are Miltonic, both in the development of the imagery and in the grand "classical" tone. Even the spondee on "daylight"— forced by the iambics surrounding it into something like reverse accent—is characteristically Miltonic. Of all poets to have on your back, Milton is the greatest poet tamer in the English language, an even more burdensome influence than Shakespeare. Reminiscing about his youthful invasion of Allen Tate's lawn, Lowell says, "My head was full of Miltonic, vaguely piratical ambitions. My only anchor was a suitcase, heavy with bad poetry. . . . I had crashed the civilization of the south."[9]

At the same time Miltown is just what it is, the thing-itself, a proper noun, contingent, profane, and utterly concrete. Yet, it is also difficult not to associate this Miltown with mill towns like Lowell, Massachusetts, with the difference between Milton, mill town, and Miltown as a measure of the distance we have fallen (from the spiritual to the material to the preventative) in the intervening centuries.

The "rising sun" in the second line suggests the *son* behind the sun; and "war paint" carries overtones of a savage sexuality which further nullifies the possibility of sex between them and prefigures the quarrel at the core of the poem. It also reminds us that one of Lowell's ancestors on his mother's side, the son of Edward Winslow, was an Indian killer ("At the Indian Killer's Grave"). The phrase "dyes us red" and its association with textile mills points back to "Where the Rainbow Ends" and the line "And I am a red arrow on this graph/ Of Revelations" (*SP* 33) and ahead toward "Skunk Hour" (*SP* 95) with its "red fox stain" and "red fire" in the skunks' moonstruck eyes.

In the poems that precede "Man and Wife" Lowell was either in McLean's or the West Street Jail—two forms of incarceration. Now he starts seeing "red" and finds himself in a murderous state in his Mother's bed. "The rising sun in war paint

dyes us red," taken as a whole line is like a kaleidoscope of crys-
tallized archetypes. Lowell hasn't tampered with the visual accuracy of the rising sun, but the line is loaded with subjective
implications conveyed entirely by linguistic means through the
juxtaposition of suggestive phrases. The phrase "Mother's bed"
reminds us that his mother is dead and that he has just escorted
her coffin across the Atlantic from Italy:

> Mother traveled first-class in the hold;
> her *Risorgimento* black and gold casket
> was like Napoleon's at the *Invalides*. . . .
> ("Sailing Home from Rapallo," *SP* 83)

Lowell's use of the phrase "broad daylight" makes us feel the
weight of their transgression "on Mother's bed," especially considering the Elizabethan meaning of "lie." And Dionysus is the
antithesis of *Miltown*, which has tamed the poet's frenzy—but
only briefly.

In the next three lines Lowell shifts from that sexually laden,
depressingly passive beginning, moves away from the clotted,
dense, claustrophobic indoor world and performs a simple act:
he looks out the window. This allows him a chance to breathe
and gives us a chance to catch our breath, grateful for the one
relaxed line we get in the poem.

> At last the trees are green on Marlborough Street,
> blossoms on our magnolia ignite
> the morning with their murderous five days' white.
> (*SP* 93)

In this antithetical image of spring and rebirth, everything is on
fire, and it isn't the first time that magnolias have incited murderous feelings in the poet.

One day when the saucer magnolias were in bloom, I bloodied
Bulldog Binney's nose against the pedestal of George Washing-

ton's statue in full view of Commonwealth Avenue; then I bloodied Dopey Dan Parker's nose; . . .

("91 Revere Street," *LS* 31)

The end of the stanza is one beautifully elongated sentence
in which Lowell recollects his first meeting with his wife-to-be,
Elizabeth Hardwick, at a literary gathering in Greenwich Village. He identifies her through her voice, just as he has previously identified his mother in "Commander Lowell." He has tried
to drink away his desire. Her voice silences him. He's on fire,
fueling the flames with alcohol, which does nothing to alleviate
his fear, "too boiled and shy/ and poker-faced to make a pass."
She is clear, all air and nerve, and brings him out of hell: the
hell of Mother's bed, the war paint, the redness. He's drawn to
her fierce intellect, her ability to scorch "the traditional South"
with words. The placement of the active verb "scorched" gives
"the shrill verve" of her "invective" the energy to actually burn
through history, to have an effect on the world. As Octavio Paz
says, "One frequently forgets that, like all other human crea-
tions, empires and states are made of words: they are verbal
acts." [10]

"Man and Wife" begins with the narrator in a vulnerable
condition; by the eighth line he's reduced to a dependency on
his wife that reenacts the relationship between mother and son.
Once again she has "dragged [him] home alive." But there are
limits to love. She needs nurturing, too, and curls up with her
back to him. Her tirade puts out the fire.

> Now twelve years later, you turn your back.
> Sleepless, you hold
> your pillow to your hollows like a child;
> your old-fashioned tirade—
> loving, rapid, merciless—
> breaks like the Atlantic Ocean on my head.

The tone at the end is deeply sorrowful and grave, like Brahms'
Four Serious Songs. The hushed, open vowels of "you hold/ your

pillow to your hollows" give us the sense that she is pressing her infant back into her in an act of self-comfort. It's as if the sound of her voice, its wavelike crescendo in the sequence "loving, rapid, merciless" has brought the whole Atlantic Ocean, into one enormous tidal wave, down on his head. The release of the accumulated force of this ocean is devastating and restorative.

The ending of "Man and Wife" unexpectedly throws us back to the sound of the ocean in "The Quaker Graveyard in Nantucket." The Atlantic ("Unmarried and corroding") has recently been connected with his mother's death; so, at the end of the poem when his wife turns the "shrill verve/ of [her] invective" on him, she has become linked, in a terrible way, with his mother. The last line has brought us full circle: back to the reverberation of the woman's voice: the mother's voice; the wife's voice. Back to the sea.

Lowell's poems have a fervent dialectic; instead of synthesis, however, they have a synaptic quality; they fill the yawning gap between the perceived and the actual; they are mental explosions. Lowell got inside the blood-curdling pith of his own life. The poems begin in grimness, in negative perception, move toward an upward resolution and then hop back—it is like what Godard referred to as tragedy in long shot—the narrator is trapped in the wake of his own poem. The world goes on after the poem is over and it is hell to fall into the world again: it is hell because it all disintegrates, digested by time.

※※※

The last poem in *Life Studies*, "Skunk Hour," (*SP* 95–96) is dedicated to Elizabeth Bishop and is, in many ways, a response to her poem, "The Armadillo," which she had dedicated to him. Lowell admired her work and saw in it a bridge between the rich texture of Dylan Thomas' language and the sparseness of

William Carlos Williams. Lowell's analysis of the composition of a Bishop poem in his review of *North & South* is just as applicable to "Skunk Hour."

> The structure of a Bishop poem is simple and effective. It will usually start as description or descriptive narrative, then either the poet or one of her characters or objects reflects. The tone of these reflections is pathetic, witty, fantastic, or shrewd. Frequently, it is all these things at once. Its purpose is to heighten and dramatize the description and, at the same time, to unify and universalize it . . . Bishop is usually present in her poems; they happen to her, she speaks, and often centers them on herself . . . her treatment of the absurd is humorous, matter of fact, and logical.[11]

Lowell's poem "Skunk Hour" is a mystery. It takes place in Castine, Maine, where Lowell spent his summers. It is a quiet New England village with graceful white frame houses, replete with churches and spires. A greening bronze statue of a musket-bearing revolutionary soldier stands in the village square. And Blue Hill looms magnificent in the distance, across the bay. It is the hill he sees in the poem, not the hill he climbs.

The poem begins with a description of the town's inhabitants: "Nautilus Island's hermit/ heiress," now "in her dotage," who thirsts for "the hierarchic privacy/ of Queen Victoria's century"; the late "summer millionaire/ who seemed to leap from an L.L. Bean/ catalogue"; the "fairy/ decorator" who "brightens his shop for fall" with a fishnet "filled with orange cork," and who discovers that, like poetry, "there is no money in his work." These figures are the poet's shadow selves. The "hermit/heiress" (note how difficult it is to read these two words as a unit so that we get the sense of her aged movements) and the reference to Queen Victoria hearken back to the "Victorian plumbing" in "Waking in the Blue," where Lowell strutted in his "turtle-necked French sailor's jersey" at McLean's, the house for mentally ill millionaires. In "Skunk Hour" the millionaire's clothing from Maine's mail order emporium connotes timelessness, durability, the intertwining of form and function, the denial of death. And so "our summer millionaire," who is portrayed here with his "nine-knot yawl" as if he had never been alive, as a cut-out, is not *dead*, he is *lost* like Warren Winslow, "dead at sea."

Tone, once again, is crucial. The narrator's disdain for these people is no more reducible to mere snobbery or prejudice than is T.S. Eliot's in his bitter caricatures of Apeneck Sweeney or Bleistein with a cigar; his disdain is an extension of his unhappy consciousness, his deeper incapacity to love himself, which is the problem he explores in the poem.

Although part of Lowell identifies with the conservative figures in the poem, he knows the old order has decayed. Senescent, it has rejected the passage of time. Lowell transforms this heritage into myth, perhaps so that he could keep it and still change. In the first poem in *Life Studies*, "Beyond the Alps," the journeying narrator, the "I," defined his position on these matters.

> I envy the conspicuous
> waste of our grandparents on their grand tours—
> long-haired Victorian sages bought the universe,
> while breezing on their trust funds through the world.
> ("Beyond the Alps," *SP* 55)

"Conspicuous waste" is incompatible with a mid-twentieth-century sensibility. No matter how difficult it may be for Lowell to relinquish his attachment to the past, his grandparents "are all gone into a world of light" and the sense of well-being he felt with them, even if experienced as pure possibility, is gone forever. In order to continue as a poet he had to relinquish some aspects of his hieratic stance. The art and the life are tied up entirely, and in making the interaction between them the actual subjects of his poems, he is forced to confront the age-old question that doesn't disappear with time, "Who am I?" The transition from the old order to the new is enacted when the millionaire's "nine-knot yawl" is "auctioned off to lobstermen," and cemented in the prosody by the deft conjunction of the sound of "yawl" with "auctioned"—the drawn out, open vowels.

Until the last line of the third stanza, "Skunk Hour" is a deceptively straightforward narrative. Havoc begins at sunset. A sour mood darkens, tarnishing the distance.

A red fox stain covers Blue Hill.

The line mixes the rusty color of stripped blueberry bushes in early fall with the color of foxes' fur and the color of dried blood. It reminds me again of the "vaguely urinous . . . Victorian plumbing" in "Waking in the Blue." And yet we are reading a poem called "Skunk Hour" and ought to be attuned to animal odors. This is the first time in the poem that Lowell interjects his own sickness: irascible, unquenchable dejection. He has all the effect of a realist and he gets us to believe, at first, that a line like "A red fox stain covers Blue Hill" is a mere objective description. It is, and we are meant to see the blueberry patches, but these images double as symbols and it is through them that he reveals the extremity of his emotional dilemma. We can never forget that Lowell writes himself into every situation. It doesn't matter to what extent this is conscious or unconscious—it is what he does; it is how he chooses to reveal himself to the world. In "Skunk Hour" the line also arrests the narrative and makes us reflect on the earlier line: "The season's ill—." Seasonal change is inevitable. Summer turns to fall and fall means the return home to the old life, which is always new and frightening upon arrival. Departure is a kind of death.

John Berryman made an heroic stab at divulging Lowell's

real intention, unearthing an answer to a question of his own invention.

> This is the poem's hard line. "A red fox stain covers Blue Hill." Even the syntax is ambiguous—the stain may be red, or it may merely be that the red foxes stain with their numbers (a plague to farmers) Blue Hill. Is the sportsman accused of having shot foxes?—but this seems sentimental and improbable; or is the fox population said to have increased since he quit shooting foxes?— but this seems even more implausible. I can't feel the implied narrative is clear. Perhaps there is no implied narrative (but shouldn't there be, tied to the millionaire as the line is?) and we have a straight dream item: for the meaning is certainly to be found in the association backward to "Spartan." This is the boy who stole a fox which, hugged to him in public, ate his vitals, the stain spreading, until stoical he fell dead; clearly a figure for the poet, still unheard of, with his growing hidden wound. At this point "Blue Hill" becomes extrageographical and macabre: the dying Spartan boy turning blue, the tall poet sad, "blue." [12]

Redness is spreading throughout the poem. It began with the "lobstermen" who bought the yawl and is reiterated in the decorator's taste for orange. But the decorator represents the opposite of the lobstermen, taking the floats used to mark their nets to decorate his shop. It would be better then for the "fairy/ decorator" to hide from his true self; he'd be better off, according to the narrator, married.

"Unmarried and corroding." Old themes. Midway through "Skunk Hour" the journey begins. The observer becomes the self-observed, and, horrified at what he has become, filled with the urge to die, and for no known reason. The tone changes from humorous to harrowing.

> One dark night,
> my Tudor Ford climbed the hill's skull;
> I watched for love-cars. Lights turned down,
> they lay together, hull to hull,

> where the graveyard shelves on the town. . . .
> My mind's not right.

"Skunk Hour" is about the pitfalls of the disjunction between the body, which is timebound and therefore doomed, and
the mind—well, all optimism falls away when it comes to the
attitude toward mind in this poem: left to its own devices it is
prone to sickness.

The view from the graveyard which overlooks the town and
the harbor, with its sailboats moored, prompts Lowell to say
that the "love-cars," those disembodied machines, "lay together,
hull to hull," tenderly, like lovers. Lowell's emphasis on "love-
cars" offers him a way out of pure voyeurism. He has other
reasons to be drawn to this scene, which bears strong resemblance to the description of the bloodless corpse in "The Quaker
Graveyard in Nantucket": "Its open, staring eyes/ Were lustre-
less dead-lights/ Or cabin-windows on a stranded hulk." That
drowned sailor was a stand-in for Lowell's cousin, Warren
Winslow, and the details of his aftermath were heavily derived
from Thoreau's *Cape Cod*. Stretching it a little, I could say that
symbolically Lowell has finally given Warren Winslow a proper
burial. This is one of Lowell's best visual echoes. These consis-
tent, recurrent subterranean core images function as a kind of
magnet. They make us linger over phrases, without quite knowing why at first, make us move backward before going ahead to
gather momentum and then they plunge us more deeply into his
dire vision—what he will come to call "the futureless future"
("Fishnet," *SP* 227).

The source of his madness is unknowable, but we can de-
tect a very special kind of tension having to do with Lowell's
attitude toward the world viewed in the poem. It's as if Lowell
constantly feels he is forbidden to do what he wants to do and,

for the most part, acts badly against his will. For example, when he writes "my Tudor Ford climbed the hill's skull," he infers that the "Tudor Ford" has taken possession of him; that it, not he, climbs "the hill's skull." The car has its own will. This is a recurring pain, or else why stress "*One* dark night." The moment the car ascends, the mind in the poem begins its descent. The rhymes, abcbca, in this stanza come full circle, just as the "hill's skull" becomes the poet's *skull;* and from here on as he journeys into the interior, the drama is the drama of his own unconscious, psychic underworld.

What he confronts in the graveyard are thoughts of his own death.

> A car radio bleats,
> "Love, O careless Love. . . ." I hear
> my ill-spirit sob in each blood cell,
> as if my hand were at its throat. . . .
> I myself am hell;
> nobody's here—

Lowell's use of the indefinite article in "A car radio bleats" underscores that this is but one of an unnamed number of cars he can't really see in the dark, and another sign of his estrangement from others. Its sounds transform the sheep on Nautilus Island into these "careless" lovers. The familiar folk song affords Lowell no relief, even adds to his distress since it suggests everything he does not have, forces him to turn inward, but he can find no comfort there either: it is as if he has been shattered into countless discrete pieces and feels the prick and sting in each blood cell. He joins body to spirit in the narrowing of the projected world into a cell. I don't know what to say about the mix of spleen and despair here except that it rages at the borderline of what is tolerable to the mind before it breaks. He is all right until he reaches a point of self-awareness in the last line of the previous stanza. It's only after he says "My mind's not right," that he turns his "ill spirit" and all the grief and rage it contains against himself.

The penultimate line of this stanza brings to mind the great dialogue between Mephistopheles and Faustus in Marlowe's tragedy. Faustus asks: "How is it then that thou art out of hell?" To which Mephistopheles replies: "Why this is hell, nor am I out of it." I said that "Skunk Hour" was a mystery. Here is my (provisional) solution. The characters in the first four stanzas are the present-day counterparts of the other people (those whom he did not choose as friends) in the book. Throughout, Lowell has been involved in a process of projection, where sometimes the borderline between self and other is blurred. The key line for our purposes is "I myself am hell." "I myself"—not the "hermit/heiress," not "our summer millionaire," not "the fairy/decorator," not, to backtrack through the book, Bobbie, Stanley, Abramowitz, or Lepke; not even his Uncle or his Aunt or his Father or his Mother: "I myself"—and it is precisely this insight that makes "Skunk Hour" a great poem, and *Life Studies* a great book rather than a collection of poems. He looks forward here to the self-reflective poems in *For the Union Dead*, *Notebook*, and *Day by Day*. In *Life Studies* Lowell has been tracking himself down, gathering evidence to account for his guilt, and he discovers that the more acutely he sees others, the same holds true for how he sees himself: unsparingly.

In Bishop's poem "The Armadillo," the imagery evolves from "the frail, illegal fire balloons" in the first stanza and proceeds with the fire balloons giving birth, as it were, to "the paper chambers," and the paper chambers giving birth to "the owl's nest" and the "glistening armadillo," who enters the poem and disappears leaving the "baby rabbit." All these images are gathered in the final chord, the *"weak mailed fist/ clenched ignorant against the sky."* [13]

And what Bishop does with imagery, Lowell does with sound—and imagery. The sheep grazing above the sea in the first stanza are transformed into sound when he hears the "car radio bleat." The "hill's skull" mirrors the chambered nautilus' shell. And when the mother skunk hunkers in at the end she *rounds*—with her wedge-head jabbed in the sour cream we see her from the neck on—and when she "drops her ostrich tail," her back arches and becomes the nautilus, the hill's skull, the outer periphery of the poet's mind.

In Lowell's work, the satanic imagination reigns. This form of aloneness ("nobody's here—") is his vision of hell. It is the dash that propels us into the next stanza, introducing, at last, the namesakes of the poem, reminding us that he does have one thing left: the power of imagination.

> only skunks, that search
> in the moonlight for a bite to eat.
> They march on their soles up Main Street:
> white stripes, moonstruck eyes' red fire

I think the best way to preface any discussion of the skunks' majestic entrance is to quote from a late essay of Lowell's where he discusses the role of *mind* in epic narrative: "mercurial and psychic . . . [if mind may be defined as a] wavering, irresistible force, a great scythe of hubris, lethal to itself, enemies and the slaves—animator of the actual." [14] At first we're not led to expect much from the appearance of the skunks in the way of enlightenment. They're doing nothing out of the ordinary, just looking for something to eat. They're not even greedy. They're the only creatures around at this hour. The skunks enact a ceremony that Lowell invests with being, fusing the supernatural and the natural in "moonstruck eyes' red fire"—as if the fire were imploding from the totality of what he has seen. The

skunks' horizontal "white stripes" mock the vertical whiteness of
the church, "under the chalk-dry and spar spire/ of the Trinitar-
ian Church." Without knowing it, they subvert the extant order
of the staid New England town—"on their soles" (I doubt they
fret or whine about the condition of their *souls*) and bring Lowell
back to his senses, put him on *his* feet.

> I stand on top
> of our back steps and breathe the rich air—
> a mother skunk with her column of kittens swills the garbage pail.
> She jabs her wedge-head in a cup
> of sour cream, drops her ostrich tail,
> and will not scare.

The purity of diction in these lines conveys the feeling of strength
through the use of such strong decisive verbs as "swills," "jabs,"
and "drops," and creates the context for the last line to have its
full impact.

The poet has come home alive, but not unscathed. The
negative energy he soaked up that caused his wounds to open
has been temporarily expelled. To accept the skunks is to accept
himself. They have power without meanness. Here are Lowell's
prefatory remarks to a reading of the poem.

> Skunk hour is the hour in the quiet of the night . . . about two
> say . . . when the garbage is out in the garbage pails and the
> skunks are out for the garbage . . . they're indomitable . . . they
> could come right through this building if there were sour cream
> or something in the garbage pail . . . they're Norman Mailer
> symbols of energy . . . hopeful symbols.
>
> *(LCR)*

In the final stanza the speaker is on his feet, slightly better
reconciled to life, able to "breathe," invigorated after this immersion in the creature world. The last line takes place in the
future tense: the movement in the poem has been from *still* to
will; from regression and stasis, toward hope. The skunks break

into the garbage and hurl Lowell out of the past into the anxious present.

❋

Let me backtrack to the beginning of this chapter. Picture for yourself each poem in the book as a mirror with writing on it. Imagine all of these mirrors lined up to reflect each other so that when you see a person or a place you also see sections of other persons and places. When you see Uncle Devereux, "as brushed as Bayard, our riding horse" (*SP* 70) you also see, in the facing mirror, "The night attendant . . . the mare's-nest of his drowsy head," (*SP* 87) and the spectrum of Ford Madox Ford as whale, "Wheel-horse," and "unforgetting elephant" (*SP* 60). When you read "blossoms on our magnolia ignite/ the morning with their murderous five days' white," (*SP* 93) you recall "*Murder Incorporated*'s Czar Lepke" who drifts "in a sheepish calm" (*SP* 92) and foreshadows the "hermit/heiress" whose sheep "still graze above the sea," (*SP* 95) who, in turn, reminds us of Commander Lowell who left the Navy "and deeded Mother his property" (*SP* 77). And we begin to see that everything in the book is linked to something which comes before or after and that it is this quality which gives the book its unity and integrity.

The transformation of raw experience into art, as Lowell practiced it, is a more radical act than it would seem and exists at a very high level of abstraction. It immediately sacrifices the universal; archetypes have to be unearthed, found amidst the myriad details of the recreated, remembered world. Lowell has been dubbed a "confessional" poet, but his is not a poetry of confession, it's a poetry of revelation. What he manages to do in the poems is not to replicate people or places as they were, but to reveal them through his feelings about them. One of the criticisms leveled against Lowell's work is that the people, places, and events alluded to in the poems are known only to him or have meaning only within a certain social-cultural milieux. But Lowell makes it clear in the poems that people like Stanley and Bobbie in "Waking in the Blue" are emblems of isolation ("more cut off from words than a seal") and he uses them to reflect the fact that the denial of the passage of time ("still hoarding the build of a boy in his twenties," "Porcellian '29") leads to psychic regression, to fantasy and madness.

There are no easy distinctions to be made here, but had Lowell wanted to change his life, his way of seeing "the new," this was the time to do so. Given the strange junctures in such poems as "Waking in the Blue," "Memories of West Street and Lepke," and "Skunk Hour," he seems ripe to lower his guard, drop his proclivity toward judgment for a while, shelve the die-hard moralist. In "Skunk Hour" he recognized the extent to which he was a victim of his own projections, that he had become the sourness that he beheld. *Life Studies* began with the disintegration of the old order and ends on the skunks, "hopeful symbols."

> When I finished *Life Studies*, I was left hanging on a question mark. I am still hanging there. I don't know whether it is a death-rope or a lifeline. Thankfully . . . the lifeline seems to me both longer and stronger than I thought at that time.[15]

ﺶﺶ

> Rejoice, my child,
> this is the untroubled instant.
> Why should I undeceive you?
> Let it not grieve you,
> if the following day is slow to arrive.
>
> ("Saturday Night in the Village,"
> *I* 28; Leopardi: *Il sabato del Villaggio*)

CHAPTER 3

The Ditch Is Nearer

We need enlarge only slightly our frame of reference to perceive that we are always moving in relation to other celestial bodies; we need merely apply time to space (travel is an illustration of this) to arrive at that traditional, and inexhaustible, metaphor of the individual life, or even all of history, as a journey from birth to death. . . . The first thing that Americans do upon walking on the moon is to raise a flag, and no one even dreams of being surprised.

—Michel Butor

Andrea: Unhappy is the land that breeds no hero.
Galileo: No Andrea, unhappy is the land that needs a hero.
—Brecht, *Galileo*

A fountain, a tower, a statue, a monument—these are the focal points in *For the Union Dead*. A statue in a square is placed where people pass by or congregate, and Lowell asks such objects to perform the same function in his book. The public artifacts have their counterparts in the private sector: a grandfather clock, a cheap toy lamp, a turtle shell, "Work-table, litter, books and standing lamp,/ plain things, my stalled equipment, the old broom—" ("Night Sweat," *SP* 134).

Most people associate Lowell with his watershed *Life Studies*. His next book of poetry, *For the Union Dead*, doesn't have the same kind of unity, but it does show development—a heightened ability to synthesize the personal with the social and historical—and it contains some of his best and most famous poems, such as the title poem and "Night Sweat." There are also a number of fine dramatic lyrics like "Water," "The Mouth of the Hudson," "The Old Flame," and "Child's Song." And then there are a number of high-pitched, headlong, quirky poems, filled with rapid shifts, questions, exclamations. Among them are "Eye and Tooth," "The Drinker," "The Neo-Classical Urn," and "Buenos Aires."

There is a radical split between the kinds of poems in the book, as if there were two minds embodied in them—a dualism between the body and the body politic. On the one hand Lowell deals with events that demand objectivity, and on the other he consciously undermines any pretense to it. In "Eye and Tooth" Lowell connects his nearsightedness with his keyhole peeping (what young boy could turn his eye away?), and thereby tries to implicate us all in a universal guilt.

> My whole eye was sunset red,
> the old cut cornea throbbed,
> I saw things darkly,
> as through an unwashed goldfish globe.
>
> My eyes throb.
>
> No ease from the eye
>
> No ease for the boy at the keyhole,
> his telescope,
> when the women's white bodies flashed
> in the bathroom. Young, my eyes began to fail.
>
> ("Eye and Tooth," *SP* 108–9)

An eye for an eye? Yes—but no more—and there is mercy in this ancient form of justice: pain is not annihilation, and Lowell can conclude the poem with a line of consummate self-negation because he has an all too human self to negate.

> I am tired. Everyone's tired of my turmoil.

But no one more than he, as everyone who cared deeply about him, especially his wife, Elizabeth Hardwick, would attest. The amount of effort it took him to struggle against his demons exhausted him. And he sought retribution for the pain he caused others through incessant poetic labor, revising endlessly, and branching out into translation and drama when his pure poetic or lyrical impulse was low. As Stanley Kunitz said in regard to his tremendous productivity, "He was indefatigable."

❧

Lowell's version of Rilke's "Self-Portrait" in *Imitations*, which was published in 1961 between *Life Studies* and *For the Union Dead*, is a powerful statement of his will to create and to overcome obstacles—none more stubborn and recalcitrant than himself:

> SELF-PORTRAIT
>
> The bone-build of the eyebrows has a mule's
> or Pole's noble and narrow steadfastness.
> A scared blue child is peering through the eyes,
> and there's a kind of weakness, not a fool's,
> yet womanish—the gaze of one who serves.
> The mouth is just a mouth . . . untidy curves,
> quite unpersuasive, yet it says its *yes,*
> when forced to act. The forehead cannot frown
> and likes the shade of dumbly looking down.
>
> A still life, *nature morte*—hardly a whole!
> It has done nothing worked through or alive,
> in spite of pain, in spite of comforting . . .

> Out of this distant and disordered thing
> something in earnest labors to unroll.
>
>   (*I* 99; Rilke: *Selbstbildnis aus dem Jahre 1906*)

The infidelities to Rilke's text, rarely felicitous ("scared," "weakness," "womanish," "forced to act"), are too numerous to mention, but Lowell's agony, his self-hatred, his hatred of his body, his misogyny, masochism, and a host of other traits that go along with his fiercely negative self-image are highlighted by such choices.

I first read Lowell's *Imitations* with careful scrutiny when I was translating Pasternak's poetry with Bohdan Boychuk. (Lowell did his imitations from other verse translations and claimed he wanted to "translate" them into English.) Given a choice between an essential and fairly general, if precise, line, image, metaphor, and an existential one, Lowell invariably chose the latter—and sometimes for good reason: to impart some quality of lived life. Because he risked making his versions seem real, and since reality in poetry had become so bound up for him with description—and a 19th-century novelist's way with detail—he lost the aura of lightness and evanescence that is crucial to the tone of a poet like Pasternak, turning a dimming lilac cluster, with its deft suggestion of dusk and an impending lightning storm into a "black scarecrow":

> The lilac bush is a black scarecrow.
>
>   ("The Seasons," *I* 139; Pasternak)

It sounds like an image out of a Roger Corman production of a Poe story, like *The Fall of the House of Usher*, or an outtake from the bleak landscape with crows in "Waking in the Blue." Pasternak's lilac is not there to keep crows away—and this internal dynamic is more crucial to the integrity of the poem than the correctness of the image. Pasternak is deft, intense, swift, painterly, and musical. (No wonder the Russians say he's untranslatable!) He concentrates on the movement and flow of the whole poem while Lowell is often—perhaps more so over time—a poet of great lines, dazzling moments, fragments.

Imitations begins with Lowell's pointed version of the first line of *The Iliad*.

> Sing for me, Muse, the mania of Achilles

Richmond Lattimore and Robert Fitzgerald, in translating the line, both use "anger."

> Sing, goddess, the anger of Peleus' son Achilleus
> (Lattimore, *The Iliad*)

> Anger be now your song, immortal one
> (Fitzgerald, *The Iliad*)

Lowell's use of the word "mania" is not only closer to the literal Greek, but also has modern clinical overtones. He must have known this. But mania is what possessed him and in using mania instead of anger Lowell is telling us something about himself as well as trying to write a good line. He wrote *Imitations* in part to reveal his deepest concerns through the work of others. These concerns are larger than the imitations themselves: they mirror prominent aspects of our age, how our culture differs—in this case—from ancient Greece.

I think of anger as an emotion that has concrete sources. Achilles' anger, directed at Agamemnon, leads to the tragic heart of that epic but it is also annealed. There is no neurosis in *The Iliad*; the directness of exchange is extremely satisfying. Achilles transcends his rage. Mania is similar in some outward aspects to anger but it admits of no specific psychological origin and heads toward no specific end. Given the growing impersonality of our societies, upwardly mobile, breeding on change, mania—along with its other half, depression—begins to supplant anger.

For the Union Dead is a response to Whitman and Baude-laire, the two pivotal poets of the nineteenth century—or to put it in Marxist terms which are equally relevant here—the state of advanced capitalism: Whitman is the hopeful vitalist, the poet of perpetual beginnings who found cosmic unity in the disparate acts he saw in a walk around the city, and who saw America, in spite of the Civil War (which he chronicled in prose journals as well as poems as he tended wounded soldiers) as the land of the future; Baudelaire is the melancholy nihilist who identified with society's outcasts, the poet who sought out the traces of the sa-cred in the lowest places, who witnessed what Walter Benjamin called "The disintegration of the aura in the experience of shock." (Rimbaud's "*Je est* un autre" is inconceivable without Baude-laire's "Hypocrite lecteur,—mon semblable,—mon frere!")

And so it is no accident that in *Imitations* there are more imitations from Baudelaire's *Les Fleurs du mal* than of any other poet. Lowell, who had just introduced new subject matter into American poetry, may have felt a particular affinity toward Baudelaire at this time. Baudelaire was the poet of that mo-ment in history when the modern world broke most brutally with its past, severed its connections. But Baudelaire did not try to subdue his language to match his subject matter. One of his pleasures (like Lowell and many other poets who were influenced by him) was to fill classical forms with modern contents, to com-bine the sonorous with the desperate, the abject, and the fabu-lous. Readers were hypnotized by the sound of the words, spell-bound by his cadences, and trapped by his luxurious syntax like flies in honey. Lowell's imitations can be read as a corrective to the Anglo-American image of him presented in earlier transla-tions. If there had been adequate versions available, I doubt he would have bothered. But it is no accident that Lowell's imita-tions, which struggle grandly to approximate Baudelaire's rhyme and meter (using iambic pentameter in place of Alexandrine) with *moments* of real success, are as far from the deeper impulse, pulse, and heartbeat of the original, and as far from the tone—the one thing Lowell claimed he wanted to maintain—as Paris is from New York or Boston.

> Stunningly simple Tourists, your pursuit
> is written in the tear-drops in your eyes!
> Spread out the packing cases of your loot,
> your azure sapphires made of seas and skies!
>
> We want to break the boredom of our jails
> and cross the ocean without oars or steam—
> give us visions to stretch our minds like sails,
> the blue, exotic shoreline of your dream!
>
> Tell us, what have you seen?
> ("The Voyage," *I* 68; Baudelaire: *Le Voyage*)

Baudelaire, like Poe whom he translated (and many would maintain "improved"), wanted to inspire horror, not, like Lowell, to shock. The grand drama of Baudelaire's poetry came from his attempt to retain that aura—that sense of the sacred in the profane—as it vanished, swallowed by the crowd.

Not every poem in *Imitations* is a *re*-translation. Lowell was one of the first to translate Eugenio Montale into English. The Montale imitations, along with those on Baudelaire, are among the most vital poems and constitute the second largest selection in the book.

> You are flung aside
> among wicker porch furniture and dank mats—
> like a water-lily dragging its roots,
> sticky, never sure-footed.
> Hysterical with life, you stretch
> towards an emptiness of suffocated sobbing.
> You are knotted in the rings of the fish-net,
> gulped by the gasping spent water . . .

Everything you grab hold of—
street, portico, walls and mirrors—
glues you to a paralysed crowd of dead things.

If a word fells you,
if a gesture ruins you now, Arsenio,
it's a sign that this is the hour for letting go
of the life you were always disposed to throttle.
A wind carries its ashes to the stars.

("Arsenio," *I* 119; Montale: *Arsenio*)

The lines I've chosen to italicize could stand as Lowell's mottoes.

Lowell was criticized for *Imitations* from the moment it was published in 1961. It marked a turning point in his career. After the acclaim he received for *Lord Weary's Castle*, and the adulation showered upon him for *Life Studies*, at the height of his reputation, he began to be attacked, knocked off his pedestal. The criticism of these imitations and other of his translations has continued.

In 1972 I attended a translation symposium at Columbia University. Lowell was not on the agenda, his work was not the topic of discussion, and to my knowledge he had not been invited to participate; yet practically everyone who spoke prefaced his talk with an offhand dismissal of *Imitations*. Most of their accusations were correct: Stephen Spender, for example, pointed out how Lowell reversed stanzas in his version of Rilke's "Orpheus, Eurydice, and Hermes." It's true: Lowell does reverse the order of stanzas, adds and deletes lines, interjects his own mood, changes the diction. And this is why Lowell called the poems "imitations." But no one was accepting his terms, and the book was treated as something morally reprehensible.

If a lesser poet had done such a book it would have gone unnoticed; but this was the act of hubris that brought the guardians of culture down on Lowell's head. It's as though they were reacting to Lowell's introductory remarks:

It seems self-evident that no professor or amateur poet, or even a good poet writing hastily, can by miracle transform himself into a fine metricist. I believe that *poetic translation*—I would call it an imitation—must be expert and inspired, and it needs at least as much technique, luck and rightness of hand as an original poem.

("Introduction," *1;* italics mine)

His biographer Ian Hamilton, even, undervalues his trilogy, *The Old Glory*, as drama, and dismisses Lowell's adaptation of Melville's novella *Benito Cereno* by quoting Melville's prose and then Lowell's free verse version, as if the evident superiority of the original as writing demonstrated the inferiority of Lowell's work—taking no account of the difference between the media.

I don't mean to imply that Lowell's versions (imitations) are in any way above criticism: they *are* criticism, not so much of the original texts, but of other and, to Lowell's way of thinking, inadequate translations. Lowell may have been too strong a poet to do translations, and if he overpowered the original, his gesture was what it was: he made the best poem in English he could from the original text. His imitations are interesting for what they reveal about him and valuable as poems, when they're good; but they're so much the product of a driven man, a single-minded, original, often maniacal poet who described his own style as rather "grisly and mechanical"; a master to be sure, but not one who, like Pound or Auden, was able to be stylistically flexible.

Given the extent to which *Life Studies* has been imitated and the fact that so much American poetry since 1960 is inconceivable without it, I think *Imitations* was justified, not morally reprehensible, and was appropriate and necessary for Lowell at that point in his career.

In *For the Union Dead* the key nonhistorical poem is "The Flaw." Lowell has a hair in his eye which throws into question all the space around him, distorts the outlines of things.

> A seal swims like a poodle through the sheet
> of blinding salt. . . .
>
> ("The Flaw," *SP* 133)

A seal doesn't swim like a poodle, but if you put a seal in such thick, crusty waters, it might swim with herky jerky movements, more frantically, like a poodle. This is a perfect example of the hallucinatory quality of Lowell's poetry, the derangement of his sense of vision—half willful, half the result of myopia and the form of madness that recurred throughout his life. His inability to see things as they are, or as they appear to others, links up interestingly to his political and historical themes.

Lowell always puts his imperfections to work for him—imperfection in the sense of Lacan's *méconnaissance*.[1] He is able to get in touch with his deepest disturbances and makes a certain kind of imperfection into a style. He is willing to stay with fleeting perceptions, resemblances—even ones he knows are not accurate.

> Bed, glasses off, and all's
> ramshackle, streaky, weird
> for the near-sighted, just
> a foot away.
>
> ("Myopia: A Night," *SP* 114)

This is Blake's crooked path to wisdom. Lowell tries to see things in a nonhabitual way. Things outside the self become the sieve, conduit, source, and storehouse of his projections.

> The light's
> still on an instant. Here
> are the blurred titles, here
> the books are blue hills, browns,
> greens, fields, or color.

                        This
is the departure strip,
the dream-road. . . .
                        ("Myopia: a Night," *SP* 114)

The tone of *Lord Weary's Castle* is one of excoriation. In *The Mills of the Kavanaughs*, a transitional book, he hones his eye to register detail, and explores the range of his capacity to invent. *Life Studies* is a refuge for him. His memories aren't pleasant, but they are his. They belong to him. Particulars mean something. They have a past. He can touch them. He is awed when he can exclaim with delight, "The farm's my own!" ("Grandparents," *SP* 74). He loved his grandfather dearly.

In *For the Union Dead* Lowell chooses to write about public experiences because they are there to be dealt with. History exists; whereas an individual has to make up his own life as he goes along. It was this structural principle that led him to republish a poem originally entitled "Colonel Shaw and the Massachusetts 54th," which appeared at the end of the 1960 Vintage paperback of *Life Studies*, as the last and title poem of *For the Union Dead*. Following hard on the heels of "Skunk Hour," Lowell must have felt that "For the Union Dead" signaled a new direction. And he placed it as the last poem in *For the Union Dead* because it gathers all the themes and variations of the poems that precede it.

> In *Life Studies* . . . I wanted to see how much of my personal story and memories I could get into poetry. . . . Afterwards, having done it, I did not have the same necessity. My new book, *For the Union Dead*, is more mixed . . . In life we speak with many false voices; occasionally, if we are lucky, we find a true one in our poems. *A poem needs to include a man's contradictions.* One side of me, for example, is a conventional liberal, concerned with causes, agitated about peace and justice and equality, as so many people are. My other side is deeply conservative, wanting

to get at the roots of things, wanting to slow down the whole
modern process of mechanization and dehumanization, knowing
that liberalism can be a form of death too. In the writing of a
poem all our compulsions and biases should get in, *so that finally
we don't know what we mean.* [2]

(Italics mine)

Lowell sounds like Simone Weil here, in his treatment of con-
tradiction as a lever of transcendence.

Where *Life Studies* received what seemed like universal ap-
preciation, the publication of *For the Union Dead* met with some
severe attacks, the fiercest one from the poet Robert Bly.

The older poets have all died in the last years; the publishing
world feels lonesome without a great poet around. Robert Lowell
is being groomed for this post. The result is evil, especially for
Lowell. . . . He is surrounded by flatterers. Moreover, one has
the sense that many of the bad poems in the book were written
to satisfy demands . . . of the alienated establishment intellectual, none of whom knows anything about poetry. . . . As we
read *For the Union Dead*, we realize that two intellectual tradi-
tions, both bankrupt, have come together in the book . . . the
value of alienation . . . [and] the notion that an artist must never
be calm, but must be *extreme* at all costs. [3]

Bly goes on to say that Lowell is "counterfeiting intellectual energy," and that his dearth of real ideas produces melodrama.
This may pertain to the bad poems in the book, most of which
Lowell had the good sense to delete from his *Selected Poems;* but
while giving credence to Bly's polemic, one has to recognize that
other factors were involved: Lowell felt the pressure of having
to live up to *Life Studies* and was aware that the move from Boston to New York would affect his writing.

There's a difference between alienation as an intellectual
construct and alienation as a state of being. Once Lowell's imagination moves out of the family and familiar terrain of *Life Studies*

there is no haven left to him. In *For the Union Dead* Lowell has "no Caribbean/ island, where even/ the shark is at home" ("Child's Song," *SP* 112). He is rootless and alone. Everything is disconnected. Only writing sustains him. "One life, one writing!" ("Night Sweat," *SP* 134). Writing is more than a partial solution to life for Lowell. He exists in and through the mirror of his words. However much he strains, plies the language, stretches, condenses, digresses or simply states, the tone is always that of a man who is writing to stay alive. And the pain never goes away. It hovers over every phrase.

> All autumn, the chafe and jar
> of nuclear war;
> we have talked our extinction to death.
>
> .   .   .
>
> Back and forth, back and forth—
> my one point of rest
> is the orange and black
> oriole's swinging nest!
>
> ("Fall 1961," *SP* 105)

"Water," the opening poem in *For the Union Dead*, takes place in "a Maine lobster town." In the poem the poet tries to make a separate peace with the world—as though following the hopeful forebodings of the skunks who "will not scare"—but he is still an alien among the inhuman surroundings. Here the men who mine the stone quarries have energy and the poet is left on shore with nothing to do but watch the sea.

> It was a Maine lobster town—
> each morning boatloads of hands
> pushed off for granite
> quarries on the islands,

> and left dozens of bleak
> white frame houses stuck
> like oyster shells
> on a hill of rock,
>
> and below us, the sea lapped
> the raw little match-stick
> mazes of a weir,
> where the fish for bait were trapped.
>
> (*SP* 99)

The first part of "Water" is neither inviting nor repelling. The details are not peculiar to the landscape; they are there. And by isolating them Lowell makes us feel the frailty and final emptiness of "unaccommodated man" face to face with the indifferent elements. It helps to keep in mind what Lowell has in mind.

> Remember? We sat on a slab of rock.
> From this distance in time,
> it seems the color
> of iris, rotting and turning purpler,
>
> but it was only
> the usual gray rock
> turning the usual green
> when drenched by the sea.

A lovely turning: after the poem has peremptorily begun, we are asked to *remember*. The poem is written in the past tense, the "remember" is purely rhetorical, yet the interrogative tone causes us to think about what has happened in the poem and what is still to come. He has been remembering, beginning with the memory of water, then he peoples it with a fragile but survival-based settlement signified by the "raw little match-stick/ mazes of a weir," and all in a kind of reverie that is not detached and vague but keen and engaged. Once the mind sets itself the task of reconstructing what the senses have perceived, the result is never merely a reproduction of reality. Through the intense shifting focus, sound, and choice of detail, the poet has created a miniature labyrinth "where the fish for bait were trapped." The "match-stick/ mazes" bring to mind associations of fire and warmth to oppose the water and the cold. It is the exile, the alien, the wanderer, who sees the strangeness in the commonplace. No longer the voyeur in the "Tudor Ford" watching for "love-cars" ("Skunk Hour," *SP* 95), Lowell needs to attain humility in the face of the elements in order to flourish on this barren seacoast where "boatloads of hands" have strength and dexterity and are there for one purpose: to cut stone.

In its way, "Water" has the rigor and precision of an experiment in perception. "From this distance in time" the poet records the distortions of memory. Here he sees that he is not the only thing that is askew. Time itself *corrodes* matter.

> The sea drenched the rock
> at our feet all day,
> and kept tearing away
> flake after flake.

And yet the sea only repeats the same action, numbing the human element. One doesn't have to be at all mad or deranged to feel pain in ordinary circumstances. The suffering in this poem is not neurotic suffering: it comes out of a basic recognition of what is there, out of the processes of nature. The rest of the poem enacts a knowing and responsive sadness.

> One night you dreamed
> you were a mermaid clinging to a wharf-pile,
> and trying to pull
> off the barnacles with your hands.

Here Lowell progresses from a deterministic attitude towards time to the timelessness characteristic of dreams and the unconscious. If their "two souls" could "return like gulls/ to the rock," it wouldn't be in this lifetime and I doubt that at this point in his life, having thrown over Catholicism, he believed it could ever happen. The "you," known to be his friend the poet Elizabeth Bishop, who dreams of being a mermaid "trying to pull/ off the barnacles," wants to be released from encrusted time. This is her assertion of the life force, a reaffirmation of the future. Each image is about something irretrievable, lost in time— the couple can't return to the rock; the past is gone; water is not their element.

> We wished our two souls
> might return like gulls
> to the rock. In the end,
> the water was too cold for us.

Memory became for Lowell what Williams wanted it to be, "a kind of accomplishment, a sort of renewal." In "The Public Garden," a beautifully paced poem, the memory of summer is prompted by the dusky autumn scene in the opening lines.

> The park is drying.
> Dead leaves thicken to a ball
> inside the basin of a fountain, where
> the heads of four stone lions stare
> and suck on empty faucets. Night
> deepens. From the arched bridge, we see

(*SP* 113)

Lowell gets grandeur into this poem without sinking it. To do this, we notice, he has to rise, climb higher, and stand on something people have made that is not grotesquely out of proportion with nature, "the arched bridge." From there, two people standing together can "see." Lowell is bound to someone else, as well as the place. It is a love poem. Throughout, the flow is gradual;

the lines are attentive to the gradient curves, nightfall, the descending thickness "in the bricky air," and have the cadence of coaches more than that of cars circling the garden, with its hidden Eden.

> Remember summer? Bubbles filled
> the fountain, and we splashed. We drowned
> in Eden, while Jehovah's grass-green lyre
> was rustling all about us in the leaves
> that gurgled by us, turning upside down . . .
> The fountain's failing waters flash around
> the garden. Nothing catches fire.

The ending of "The Public Garden" is an adaptation of some fine lines from "The Mills of the Kavanaughs" in the book of the same title:

> Here bubbles filled
> Their basin, and the children splashed. They died
> In Adam, while the grass snake slid appalled
> To summer, while Jehovah's grass-green lyre
> Was rustling all about them in the leaves
> That gurgled by them turning upside down;
> The time of marriage!—
>
> *(The Mills of the Kavanaughs, p. 85)*

In spite of his use of the third person here, the underlying experience was his; in "The Public Garden" he claims it. The juxtaposition of these two passages exemplifies the way in which Lowell's treatment of subject matter and personal experience changed from his early to middle work. It is this treatment, with its emotional pressure (compare "We drowned/ in Eden" with "They died/ In Adam") and its associative leaps ("the fountains' failing waters" and "Nothing catches fire" bring to mind the passing of youth and the end of the romance alluded to earlier in the poem), that makes Lowell's poetry *modern*.

When we speak of modern art we speak of the treatment of

a subject (cubism, dadaism), the process of inquiry, the blurring of time, the obliteration of the subject, the exploration of material rather than commentary. As Thomas Hess says of the painter Willem de Kooning, and other abstract expressionists, they

> changed the basic hypothesis of art. It can be described (in a simile) as a shift from aesthetics to ethics; the picture was no longer supposed to be Beautiful, but True—*an accurate representation or equivalence of the artist's interior sensation and experience*. If this meant that a painting had to look vulgar, battered, and clumsy—so much the better.[4]

Beginning with the poems in "Life Studies" Lowell uses the techniques of modern art with its shape shifting, its modes of memory and time juggling; his poems no longer arrive at any resolution or answer to any of the questions or problems, no matter how provisional. The end of *Lord Weary's Castle* was hopeful insofar as it posited a future.

> What can the dove of Jesus give
> You now but wisdom, exile? Stand and live,
> The dove has brought an olive branch to eat.
> ("Where the Rainbow Ends," *SP* 33)

And the ending of "Thanksgiving's Over" from *The Mills of the Kavanaughs*, no matter how bleak, was definite,

> I sat. I counted to ten thousand, wound
> My cowhorn beads from Dublin on my thumb,
> And ground them. *Miserere?* Not a sound.
> ("Thanksgiving's Over," *SP* 51)

when compared with the later poems:

> I hold an *Illustrated London News*—;
> disloyal still,
> I doodle handlebar
> mustaches on the last Russian Czar.
> ("Grandparents," *SP* 75)

I keep no rank nor station.
Cured, I am frizzled, stale and small.
                    ("Home After Three Months Away," *SP* 90)

꧂꧂

The tone of *For the Union Dead* darkens progressively. The
poems are catalogues of inconsolable anguish: the present scene
seen as a nightmare. It is as if he did not want to make it back
from willed regression to childhood in *Life Studies*, and sees all
change as change for the worse. In "The Drinker" Lowell reg-
isters the vengefulness of inanimate objects ("Stubbed before-
breakfast cigarettes/ burn bull's eyes on the bedside table") and
the vengefulness of his body and mind in taut, desperate images.

> The man is killing time—there's nothing else.
> No help now from the fifth of Bourbon
> chucked helter-skelter into the river,
>
> .   .   .
>
> No help from his body, the whale's
> warm-hearted blubber, foundering down
> leagues of ocean, gasping whiteness.
> The barbed hooks fester. The lines snap tight.
>
> (*SP* 116)

Notice the significant echo of the fifth section of "The Quaker
Graveyard in Nantucket": the transformation into the whale, a
mammal that needs both elements, water and air, to survive.

The relationship of this drinker to his absent wife is re-
markably similar to that of the Consul and Yvonne in Malcolm
Lowry's novel *Under the Volcano*. The Consul is the drinker of
drinkers: drinking has become his vocation, even supplanting his
wife whom he still loves. And the thought that she hates him,
hates him as much for what he has done to himself as for the

pain he has inflicted directly on her, is intolerable. His agony precedes what he perceives. His own judgment of himself—that he is guilty, ontologically guilty—makes him read *her signs* as an indictment.

> He looks at her engagements inked on her calendar.
> A list of indictments.
> At the numbers in her thumbed black telephone book.
> A quiver full of arrows.

He gives the motive for his mood, reveals the modus operandi of the poem. He is going through her things looking for evidence to give credence to his suspicions, his jealousy. "The barbed hooks fester. The lines snap tight," echoes his suicidal mood in "Waking in the Blue": "My heart grows tense/ as though a harpoon were sparring for the kill" (*SP* 87). This clearly feels worse than "A list of indictments. . . . A quiver full of arrows," especially to one who already has been wounded, who has already fallen, who feels as though he were trapped and gashed underwater.

In his hungover despair she could have wooed even the vermin away. Sounds are Lowell's weapons and he releases these venomous sibilants against her for leaving him alone. "Her absence hisses like steam, . . . [He] hears the voice of Eve,/ . . . No voice/ outsings the serpent's flawed, euphoric hiss." But at this thought his grisly sense of humor returns: "The cheese wilts in the rat-trap,/ the milk turns to junket in the cornflakes bowl." By the last stanza the poem and the poet are saved. His gaze turns outward.

> Is he killing time? Out on the street,
> two cops on horseback clop through the April rain
> to check the parking meter violations—
> their oilskins yellow as forsythia.

This is different in tone from any preceding stanza. He has begun to take delight in sight and sound again. The second line is perfect onomatopoeia. And where "his distracted eye" had seen "only glass sky" now he is able to focus and see "oilskins yellow as forsythia."

I think that Lowell felt his mania to be a kind of drunkenness. William James wrote about the drinker as a failed religious man or mystic who turns to the bottle for inspiration. And this poem, "The Drinker," makes me think of Malcolm Lowry's apologia for alcohol in a letter to his publisher-to-be explaining the structure of *Under the Volcano* and the meaning of the theme:

> In the Cabbala, the misuse of magical powers is compared to drunkenness or the misuse of wine, and termed, if I remember rightly, in Hebrew *sōd*. . . . There is a kind of attribute of the word sod also which implies garden or a neglected garden . . . for the Cabbala is sometimes considered as the garden itself, with the Tree of Life, which is related of course to that Tree the forbidden fruit of which gave one the knowledge of good and evil, and ourselves the legend of Adam and Eve, planted within it. Be these things as they may—and they are certainly at the root of most of our knowledge, the wisdom of our religious thought, and most of our inborn superstitions as to the origin of man—William James if not Freud would certainly agree with me when I say that the agonies of the drunkard find their most accurate poetic analogue in the agonies of the mystic who has abused his powers.[5]

Lowell's "drinker," like Lowry's Consul, is guilty of some unnameable sin and damned to begin with; writing of this sort is psychological excavation, an attempt to retrieve the buried self, unleash blocked energy.

※

In "The Neo-Classical Urn" (*SP* 125), Lowell identifies the object of his guilt, but more importantly the poem is about the route to poetry—with its detours, gauntlets, impasses, and ele-

mental cruelty. It is a short narrative poem which lurches as the
poet's body lurches, in search of rest. "Rest!/ I could not rest!"
This is the kind of poem that shows Lowell at his best and most
himself—onstage, offstage, arguing with others, arguing with
himself, and all in the same hybrid lyric. He makes a connection
with his animal self in the first line, and to understand what
ensues we must note that the narrator is possessed when he rubs
his head and finds instead a "turtle shell/ stuck on a pole," finds
it is the shell that drives the head, "each hair electrical/ with
charges, . . . always purposeful . . ./ Poor head!" Lowell is a
skeptic with pantheist tendencies, and would exclaim with Keats:
"O for a life of sensations rather than thoughts." This is why he
envied creatures and why there are so many of them in his
poems.

The poet soon discovers he has always been driven in this
way, that he and the turtle shell, remainder and reminder of the
turtles he once killed, are one: "In that season of joy,/ my turtle
catch/ was thirty-three"—a very Christian number.

The further off in time and memory, the stranger and more
complicated the memories become. "At full run on the curve" is
clear enough, but the perfection of the colonnade's "cylindrical/
clipped trunks *without a twig between them*" (italics mine) is dis-
rupted, and the fantasy of order turns into its opposite once he
spins past the grotesque "statue" of a nymph who levitates and
titillates and interrupts his headlong run. He bogs down, "the
pathway now a dyke," and reaches an impasse with hints of a
gauntlet.

The second and last stanza begins with a series of exclamations and shifts briefly from the first person to the third. He
sees his boyhood self in the third person because "The boy was
pitiless who strummed/ their elegy." Why? Because he still feeds
on their death which, given the unambiguous connection, is
symbolically his own. The adult's sense of mortality erodes the
omnipotence of childhood. The poem ends:

> What pain? A turtle's nothing. No
> grace, no cerebration, less free will
> than the mosquito I must kill—
> nothings! Turtles! I rub my skull,
> that turtle shell,
> and breathe their dying smell,
> still watch their crippled last survivors pass,
> and hobble humpbacked through the grizzled grass.
>
> ("The Neo-Classical Urn," *SP* 126)

This is the return of what was repressed. Lowell killed these turtles thoughtlessly in an act of boyhood sadism, and now they've possessed him, and "their dying smell," still present in his nostrils, forces him to recognize the meaning of that unconscious act. As a child, he denied the possibility of pain in beings without consciousness, "no cerebration."

The past and present commingle in the last three lines. He watches the turtles move off with a burst of affection and easy alliteration which works because the voice is playful and the rest of the poem is so racked and spasmodic. We're grateful for some resolution and the appearance of the "crippled last survivors," who, in a playful echo of Keats' "hare [that] limped trembling through the frozen grass" in "The Eve of Saint Agnes," "hobble humpbacked through the grizzled grass."

The self-conscious alliteration is a device that recurs in several significant poems in *For the Union Dead*. And its effect is complex. First, it draws our attention to language, delays the forward movement of the action, and the sound overwhelms the image. If we were to take out "humpbacked" and "grizzled," words which are not necessary to convey the image (Williams would have left them out), the line would have an entirely different tone. It would be sad and border on pathos instead of being somewhat humorous and affectionate. No matter how closely any poem resembles experience, there's no escape from questions of language when talking about poetry. In such a context, Lowell's line, its wordplay and hyperbole, comments on the existing state of the English language, explores its possibilities, and reminds us through language that words are words and things are things and that there is not a *natural* congruence between them.

❦

In *For the Union Dead*, Lowell becomes a walker in the city, in cities, and I want to say (to extend the comparison with Baudelaire) a *flâneur*. Several poems take place in cities away from home: "Florence," "July in Washington," and "Buenos Aires." But the furthest and deepest dislocation occurs in the move from Boston to New York. In New York Lowell thought himself to be "on the firing line."

> Now the midwinter grind
> is on me, New York
> drills through my nerves,
> as I walk
> the chewed-up streets.
>
> ("Middle Age," *SP* 103)

Where to find comfort then, if not here? "Buenos Aires"? He goes there, as to Washington, in an official capacity. But the man could soak up the anger of a place like a sponge from which he merely had to squeeze the content.

> In my room at the Hotel Continentál

Now that's an intriguing beginning. The reader doesn't know whether or not the hotel was really called the "Hotel Continentál" but it's (a) not unlikely, and (b) perfect. There are Hotel Continentals in every major city and they range from stage sets with signs to lavish palaces with awnings and doormen.

A local name for such a hotel would not do. Lowell's use of proper nouns is multidimensional. Sometimes, as is often the case with Whitman and Williams, he uses them because they are there to be used. At other times, such as this one, Lowell makes an implicit social and moral commentary on the modern will to be assimilated through the anonymity created by the use of a stereotypical name, as if the place name had an existence apart from its concrete reality.

"Buenos Aires" is a good poem to examine in detail because here Lowell is far from home and most susceptible to the feelings of repugnance, disgust, anger, and dislocation which any sensitive traveler might share. The first stanza of "Buenos Aires" is one of Lowell's strangest, strongest, and truest beginnings. Often he needs time to gain momentum; here he begins with it.

> In my room at the Hotel Continentál
> a thousand miles from nowhere,
> I heard
> the bulky, beefy breathing of the herds.
>
> (*SP* 128)

The man is alone and anxious. So what does he do next, as befits our consumer society? Goes shopping.

> Cattle furnished my new clothes:
> my coat of limp, chestnut-colored suede,
> my sharp shoes
> that hurt my toes.

Nothing fits. His new shoes are too narrow for his feet, a significant detail since he is about to explore the city on foot. History will not give him the chance to participate directly in events. The best he can do is bear witness.

In the second stanza he puts himself in the role of the guilty bystander. "When in Rome. . . ." Always in Lowell's poetry the extremity of the outer situation helps to balance and counteract his tendency to self-flagellation. Give him an ordinary Boston morning; give him time on his hands—time to tally up his endless "sins"—and he will project his own accumulated revulsion onto anything that enters his line of vision. But give him an externally difficult and complex circumstance to cope with and he will stay with the pain all the way through without wincing. In the next six stanzas he walks around, quietly observing. He doesn't like what he sees: the results of Perón's military dictatorship. A hush in the city. A reined-in feeling.

> A false fin de siècle decorum
> snored over Buenos Aires
> lost in the pampas
> and run by the barracks.

And the tight-lipped quality of the first line, leaving no room for breath, has evolved right out of the "sharp shoes/ that hurt my toes." There had just been a military coup in Brazil and Argentina was feeling the pinch. It was tending in that direction, too, "lost in the pampas/ and run by the barracks"—which is to say that life goes on—and nothing less than a gun at the head will make a man give up his siesta.

> and run by the barracks.

Lowell makes the soldiers sound as directionless and complacent as everyone else he sees and, mainly, *does not see* while in town. The soldiers have a job to do, but they are the mere instruments of power. "The barracks," of course, don't run anything, they merely house the military.

What's the most natural thing for the weary traveler to do next? Take refuge in the news.

> All day I read about newspaper coups d'état
> of the leaden, internecine generals—
> lumps of dough on the chessboard—and never saw
> their countermarching tanks.

But the news, of course, affords no refuge. And the effect of this quick phantomlike global communication on the individual psyche is an issue that Lowell broaches throughout this book. If World War II was, in its way, the subtext for the apocalyptic tone of *Lord Weary's Castle*, the "news" has much the same role in *For the Union Dead*. "All autumn, the chafe and jar/ of nuclear war;/ we have talked our extinction to death" ("Fall 1961," *SP* 105). The poem, "Alfred Corning Clark," which is a life study but wouldn't have fit into *Life Studies* (an assertion I make because there are no other poems in that book dedicated to any friends whose role in Lowell's life preceded his choice of vocation), begins "You read the *New York Times*/ every day at recess" (*SP* 110).

Lowell renders the experience of getting the news like a negative infusion. The "newspaper coups d'état" are unsettling but not quite real. There are few experiences in the so-called normal course of daily life that are as unsettling as this, and Lowell is willing to explore the consequences of receiving information second-hand from the news media with their pseudo-objectivity. (He even ends the book getting the news from that other, newer, ubiquitous and consuming medium, the television.) Lowell implies that the newspaper makes the event seem distant—and in this case more distant than it is, given his immediate proximity to Brazil—(where the coup d'état has occurred). Nor can I think of anything more insidious than "leaden, internecine generals" who propagate death and destruction only, and devour themselves along with the others: the enemy.

Lowell's vision of nature and his vision of history collide here. He finds the same brutal dualities in such things as "countermarching tanks" as in the process of creation:

> When the Lord God formed man from the sea's slime
> And breathed into his face the breath of life,
> And blue-lung'd combers lumbered to the kill.
> > ("The Quaker Graveyard in Nantucket," VII, *SP* 10)

Lowell is existential *and* determinist—sometimes in the same poem. But the weight of history is a constant pressure and reminder of that freedom, which, if it exists at all, exists in context. Lowell arrives at this conviction through experience. His vision of history, whatever its limits, is in the best sense earned. This belief in context has a function in Lowell's work similar to Blake's insistence on "minute particulars." It is also paralleled by Pasternak's assertion that although the afterlife is still a riddle, life could be defined through details.

We left him in "Buenos Aires" reading the newspaper. In the next stanza we find him:

> Along the sunlit cypress walks
> of the Republican martyrs' graveyard,
> hundreds of one-room Roman temples
> hugged their neo-classical catafalques.

This is a strangely passive construction for Lowell, and perfect for a poem in which history, current and ancient, overwhelms the individual. He uses the first person sparingly and to great effect. "Walks" not only rhymes with "catafalques" and makes a jarring, bizarre connection click, it also clarifies his intentions. Lowell sees three stages of history in collision. And the "sunlit cypress walks" are the only untainted, beautiful things in the poem. Nature is benign and quiet—and presides over the dead. The sudden gentleness here prefigures the treatment of nature in "Soft Wood" and in his late book of love poems, *The Dolphin*.

The rest of the world he sees around him, a world which has been created by men, is a series of false fronts. Architecture reflects the spirit of a people. Certain styles and cultures do not mix. They produce hybrid uglinesses. The "Roman temples" and "neo-classical catafalques" are poorly grafted onto the landscape. And when Lowell uses "hugged" to join these two gloomy partners, it is a complex and decisive gesture. The word works at so many levels of meaning and significance while retaining its basic thrust. This is another instance of what I mean when I say that Lowell continually explored the possibilities of language.

> Literal commemorative busts
> preserved the frogged coats
> and fussy, furrowed foreheads
> of those soldier bureaucrats.

Lowell does here with "literal" what he does with "hugged" in the preceding stanza; he turns the word against itself. His use of "literal" may rouse him and cause him to stretch that aspect of the poem in the next stanza—especially since he's kept so close to the facts. "Literal," in this context, becomes *allied to evil*. And what more bitter criticism could be leveled against Lowell as a poet but that he was *too* literal, that he stayed too close, clung too tenaciously, to surfaces; that he had inherited the Puritan's mistrust of the imagination.

Lowell doesn't often rein in his anger. These tight quatrains are just right. He tried not to go wild "a thousand miles from nowhere," and the need for self-control may be the organic source of the form. The word "preserved" is turned against itself too. It reads more like *embalmed*. During a time when South American governments were being overthrown—changing hands—it is appropriate that this historically minded poet would seek out the signs that led to decay, and to the extent that the fault lies with government, "those soldier bureaucrats" in "frogged coats" and "fussy, furrowed foreheads," Lowell's contempt seems justified. In "July in Washington" he unleashes another torrent of rage and indignation.

> On the circles, green statues ride like South American
> liberators above the breeding vegetation—
>
> prongs and spearheads of some equatorial
> backland that will inherit the globe.

(*SP* 127)

What Lowell sees in the signs he chooses to show us is the travesty of history. The irritable *f* sounds, which we will hear later ("finned cars nose forward like fish"), running together in hideous alliteration, mirror his sense of the place accorded the "soldier bureaucrats" on the evolutionary ladder. The "frogged coats" make me think of men who, barely emerged from the swamp, immediately don the French style of dress and reign with all the empty authority that is available to those who know that "clothes make the man." Lowell's attentiveness to surfaces may be a limitation but it is never superficial. The busts' expression ("fussy, furrowed foreheads") also indicates anxiety and uncertainty about how to look dignified, like the French kings.

Anyone who is not sympathetic to Lowell's enterprise or attuned to his sense of humor might think of the penultimate stanza of "Buenos Aires" as downright pathetic.

> By their brazen doors
> a hundred marble goddesses
> wept like willows. I found rest
> by cupping a soft palm to each hard breast.

Until this stanza the poem has systematically built a case against everything it has encountered. There were "hundreds of one-room Roman temples," enough to daze the brain. But "a hundred marble goddesses" is within the body's range. That they "wept like willows" is Lowell's way of saying that he would say anything that might humanize the heated scene he's been thrown into. The observer in him sees "brazen doors" and he needs more now than another coy façade.

Relief is in sight and mind but there's a catch. It's time for another assault on the inanimate. The "marble goddesses" have no life in them because they are not and never were alive. He envisions a harem. And yet, through the alchemy of poetry, it seems natural that the marble goddesses "wept like willows" and are ultimately more human than anything that preceded them in the poem. This poet, the agent of this vision, witnesses the event.

The last line and a half are more questionable. I don't know quite how to take them. If the intent were manifest in the end rhymes, "rest"/"breast," I would feel that the poem had worked through to an admission of need, blatant, raw, and primitive at root: qualities Lowell could transform into poetry rather than obstacles to be averted. But when Lowell resorts to "cupping a soft palm to each hard breast," I feel he's posing, that he's stepped outside and taken a snapshot of himself. The "I," who now appears to act for the first time in the poem retreats into a kind of self-watchfulness. And he does something to astonish the crowd of imagined onlookers. We have heard from this "I" before, in the first and fourth stanza: "I heard," and "I read," is what it said. Is there some perverse ratio in Lowell between clarity of action and meaning? Is this least suggestive and metaphysical line in the poem also, by hook and crook, the most opaque? Clearly he doesn't touch the "hard breast" of the "*hundred* marble goddesses." Does the *thought* of real women's flesh help him find rest? The last stanza belies such conjecture.

> I was the worse for wear,
> and my breath whitened the winter air
> next morning, when Buenos Aires filled
> with frowning, starch-collared crowds.

He feels like flayed cattle here, his outer, protective covering has been removed. He has been too much with the world. But the staunch witness remains at the end to capture the discomfort of the city's citizens. The citizens are "frowning" because their lives are not in their hands. The stiff, rigid, "starch-collared crowds," however, were that way before, aspiring to a higher order: the standard of living of the middle class in America. They're "frowning" because of the "coups d'état" and the instability of the state.

The thing to keep in mind about such an overtly political poem as "Buenos Aires" is that Lowell, after once again registering the feeling in the air, goes on to transform imaginatively his persona into a voice that mirrors the scene perceived. The feeling of constriction derived from the suppression of free speech and in particular from the "coups d'état" that supplanted the Mussoliniesque Perón is rendered through such images as "sharp shoes/ that hurt my toes." Lowell makes a point of rendering his own instinctive reaction before speaking for the people, the "frowning, starch-collared crowds" who are forced by the military dictatorship to live without freedom, to revolt, or to die.

❧

I have talked about "Buenos Aires" in detail because there's been so much fervent debate about political poetry and I think that Lowell avoids all of the obvious pitfalls—the most blatant of which is generalization. I think that his capacity to write good political poetry is intimately connected both to his obsession with history and his place in it. Lowell saw politics as an aspect of daily life. This is rare in America, where politics is associated with government, and government—prior to Vietnam and Watergate—is something with an aura of holiness and untouchability about it.

Such is not at all the case in countries with longer histories. Europeans are quick to respond to any decision made for them by government and fierce in argument no matter what their social class. In America, to use one of Lowell's favorite words, people are "cowed." I remember in 1980 hearing the father of one of the hostages being held in Iran interviewed on television. The newscaster asked him how he felt about President Carter's decision to cut off diplomatic relations with Iran after the hostages had already been held for half a year. The man was absolutely reluctant to criticize the President. He did his level best to put his personal feelings to the side. An extraordinary attitude in itself! He sounded like the most decent, fair-minded man you would ever care to meet. And the newscaster had to coax him out of the total mental separation he had made between his feelings about his son's captivity and his sense of government as something innately good. He said he was sure that the President was doing all that he could, but when asked if he thought America should have cut off diplomatic relations with Iran before half a year had gone by, his whole tone changed. He hesitated, stammered, and then said, with visible relief, "yes, yes, I think he should have done it months ago." The newscaster gently probed a little further. Did he think that Carter's decision in this election year might be political? His second "yes" caught in his throat again. He digressed, said he had met Mr. Carter, thought he was an honest man and that he was doing his best, but that *"yes, yes, I would have to say yes, that politics was a factor in Carter's decision."* (He was interviewed by phone. We could not see his face.) He was clearly relieved (from the tone of his voice) to get this off his chest, but I also felt that he thought he had blasphemed, and that it hurt him and jarred his own sense of reality, as might be the case with a Christian who discovers, after a devout life, that he doesn't believe, say, in the Virgin birth.

It's likely that a Frenchman, from a comparable social class, would explode with such scatalogical caterwaulings that they would never reach our ears for bleeping. And when I read foreign poets like Montale (whom Lowell vigorously translated), Pavese, Follain, Ritsos, and Tranströmer (to touch merely on Italy, France, Greece, and Sweden), I feel that the personal and the political are integrated, and that there is no irritable straining for connections between the two—since they are one. They *are* one. And these poets may not have had to think twice about it. The same kind of linkage occurs in Blake's "Auguries of Innocence," when he puts it (ever so succinctly):

> A dog starv'd at his Master's Gate
> Predicts the ruin of the State.[6]

Or, more germane to Lowell's practice, in "London":

> And mark in every face I meet
> Marks of weakness, marks of woe.
>
> .   .   .
>
> But most thro' midnight streets I hear
> How the youthful Harlot's curse
> Blasts the new-born Infant's tear,
> And blights with plagues the Marriage hearse.[7]

If the attitude of the hostage's father toward government is typical in this country—and I think it is—and if most American poets grow up in such an atmosphere—and I think they do—then it's no wonder that so much political poetry attempted by many of our better poets sounds strained.

Lowell immersed himself in history from the start and took it for his theme, which kept him out of uncharted waters and let him take aim at extant tradition. I don't think that *For the Union Dead* is any more political than his earlier books. It is only so on the surface and because it deals more with surfaces. Current events. The infiltration of daily life by the media. What gives the book integrity, in contrast to the internal, structural unity we find in *Life Studies*, is Lowell's insistence that the personal poems, whose core images are based on "the flaw" and which trace the ramifications of subjectivity, are no less *political* than their counterparts. The structure of the book is a corrective to the way of thinking about politics that we have inherited. Is private life ever any less political than public life?

I don't think that political concerns have to manifest themselves in the overt subject matter of a poem or any work of art. A work of art is political when it connects the individual and the *polis*. It is not unlikely that true concern is political in itself because the individual is part of the polis and the quality of his attention has content, and by extension, meaning, which may very well stand at some variance with intention. In so many poems that fail as art you hear the voice of the teller imposing his will on the material. I don't think that politics should be left to causes and I'm more interested in *how* Lowell says what he says than in *what* he says. But this in no way invalidates his politics or his political poetry. There is more than one way to bear witness. If we begin as political beings then everything we think and do has political implications. But artists often find no solution (or prospective solution) within the political realm and it is possible that the recognition of the absence of any solution may be the fiercest prod to continued thought, art, and action.

❦

The real subject of the book, the common bond, is pain, as Geoffrey Hartman perceived:

> Lowell . . . associates birth with labor and violence. Things 'bleed with dawn'. . . . The major concern of this book is, as ever, pain: pain and anguish at temporality. . . . Lowell's attitude toward time is paradoxical: time is the accuser, yet time is inauthentic. Time eyes us through objects that loom large, or through "unforgivable" landscapes, yet everything converges to no effect, like waves breaking harmlessly and sight blurring.[8]

When I first read "New York 1962: Fragment" I couldn't locate its interior, and with lines like "still over us our breath/ sawing and pumping to the terminal," and then "two in one waterdrop/ vitalized by a needle drop of blood," I thought Lowell meant the "two" were in the hospital. Earlier in the book, in "Florence," Lowell, borrowing an image from Mary McCarthy's *The Stones of Florence*, had written that "the tower of the Old Palace/ pierces the sky/ like a hypodermic needle" (*SP* 106), and though the simile itself is weak and inappropriate in this context, both too obvious and too private, it helps explain why I or any reader might feel that the couple in "Fragment" is in the hospital. Lowell's dread of hospitals and hypodermics (with their implications of transfusions and injections) imbues the room with some of this feeling of stifled air. His displacement of images which haunt him confuse and perplex the reader as well as enrich the poem.

In "New York 1962: Fragment" (*SP* 132), the context is implied, not specified.

> This might be nature—twenty stories high,

The word "might" immediately identifies the context as hypothetical, not actual—calling into question the relationship of nature to the human in the cityscape. Here the city scene is seen as a mutation of nature, in an odd juxtaposition of city and country:

> two water tanks, tanned shingle, corseted
> by stapled pasture wire, while bed to bed,

then he incarnates the metaphysical in the physical fact—

> we two, one cell here, lie
> gazing into the ether's crystal ball,

from which we can deduce two lovers, man and wife (note the affinity between this poem and "Man and Wife"), and see them looking out of the window:

> sky and a sky, and sky, and sky, till death—
> my heart stops. . . .

Are the "two water tanks" symbols of themselves, in separate beds, yet "one cell here," together and apart, as if anyone could escape double solitude? Or is the crystal ball the other lover's eye? Or his or her deeper "I"? Are they making love and staring into each other's eyes? It is clearly unclear.

> This might be heaven. Years ago,
> we aimed for less and settled for
> a picture, out of style then and now in,
> of seven daffodils. We watched them blow:

The inanimate which comes to life reactivates the past. Winds of memory stir the memory, whereas the immediate sky or the eye, those objects of the present tense, deaden it. I especially like the relaxed tone of the impossible assertion, "We watched them blow," as if it were utterly natural for flowers on canvases to blow (as it is for figures on a frieze to move). And to turn the inside of this room into the outside—field or meadow—in order to recall earlier and better times, flames of love in the heat of summer, when their life force was stronger, "high summer in the breath that overwhelms/ the termites digging in the under-pinning. . . ."

But the past remains, "Still over us, still in parenthesis," like the frame of the painting, suspended; and the "two" referred to in Lowell's poem are not patients in any literal sense but rather intimates, (and/or inmates in their cell), lovers engaged in the act of love through phases of lull, spasm, and orgasm, and the ending echoes a line in "The Mills of the Kavanaughs" (quoted earlier in regard to "The Public Garden"): the repetition of down—"down, down, down, down," counterpointed in "New York 1962: Fragment" by the fervent "up, up, up, up and up,/ soon shot, soon slugged into the overflow/ that sets the wooden workhorse working here below." And yet, the sense we get is still one of confinement and direness: we are confined to our bodies, our cells, ourselves.

Baudelaire's poem "Anywhere Out of the World" is the definitive ironic statement of this theme of confinement and its concomitant attributes: the fantasy of escape, the desire to be anywhere but where you are at any moment in time, and the feeling that life, "high summer," is always where you are not. We know of Lowell's immersion in Baudelaire through his translations, and though he wasn't interested in translating prose poems, I think that this one is closer to his heart than any of those he put into English.

> Life is a hospital where each patient is obsessed by the desire to change beds. This one would like to suffer in front of the stove, that one thinks that he would recover in front of the window. It seems to me that I shall always be comfortable wherever I am not, and that question of moving is a ceaseless topic of discussion with my soul.[9]

Politics and dailiness. The individual on the stage of history. How the public world impinges. Lowell's desire to write public poetry. His need to confront history, especially American history. The fact of "The Public Garden" just being there. The phenomenon of public places. What was given him to write and what he felt compelled to write about. Much of the suffering enacted in the poems results from the fact that Lowell was caught between the new order and the old, as beautifully exemplified in his impromptu, prefatory remarks to a reading of his poem, "For the Union Dead," in 1960.

> For some reason, the last war doesn't seem to have inspired monuments. . . . We've emerged from the monumental age . . . I can't think of any in Boston. One thing we did have . . . was a rather beautiful, strange photograph of something mushrooming into the air. . . . It was Hiroshima and it was an advertisement

for Mosler Safes. One of them survived the blast. Our culture's indestructible.

(LCR)

The nature of modern warfare is such that individual heroism is relegated to being a private act, which may be why the statues of World War II are of the Unknown Soldier. And the atomic bomb is the ultimate depersonalized weapon. "For the Union Dead" was written at the peak of the Cold War, at the beginning of the Civil Rights Movement, and almost one hundred years after the Civil War. A synthesis of these factors, the poem proposes some alternatives to the utterly fragmented, decadent world that Lowell has portrayed in the book. By "some alternatives" I don't mean anything like easy solutions. Like a symphony after a series of sonatas, the poem ends with a more consummate negation, through statement and implication, than any of the other poems; it has some forceful, positive strands, some hopeful, uplifting sounds. In it the personal and the political are carefully interfused.

"For the Union Dead" has a subject: freedom, rebellion versus servility. The pivot or formal axis of the poem is "St. Gaudens' shaking Civil War relief,/ propped by a plank splint against the garage's earthquake" (*SP* 135). Lowell breathes life into the statue and sets the rage that he feels in opposition to the unnatural, machinated violence that sunders the air. A "plank splint" is all that stands—symbolically—between two centuries, two historical eras.

Where the other people—outside the family—in *Life Studies* were mainly literary, in *For the Union Dead* he moves more and more toward the historical. Writing well is no longer sufficient justification for a life. Lowell, like Byron in *Don Juan*, wants a hero. Unlike Byron, however, he wants a hero capable of political commitment, action, a man with whom he can feel some affinity. And he discovers him right on his home ground, in the monument on Boston Common. As Lowell remarked:

It's a good deal of embarrassment if you're a New Englander that the writing in the south has been so superior to ours in this century I think . . . they . . . go to town on the Civil War . . . and many of my closest friends have been southerners . . . and we've had this bone to pick between us . . . this is a very key subject that I'm writing on . . . there was a young man in Boston named Robert Gould Shaw . . . he was the sort of young man who would have known Emerson . . . not exactly an intellectual himself but knew that world . . . and he was asked to command the first Negro regiment and that was quite a risky thing to do.

(LCR)

Shaw's endangered immortality, "the shaking Civil War relief," prompts Lowell to tell Shaw's story. But the poem begins with an observation about the neglect of the "old South Boston Aquarium," one of Lowell's childhood haunts. The Boston Common is a ten minute walk from 91 Revere Street, where Lowell lived as a boy. He probably passed it every day. No matter how public a statement the poem makes, its focus is personal and specific: his garden is being torn up. And it is this private sadness that distinguishes it from other poems in the same genre.

This poet, whose *I* found its greatest solidity in childhood and whose imagination has been most powerfully engaged by the sea, joins these two concerns in the first two stanzas.

> The old South Boston Aquarium stands
> in a Sahara of snow now. Its broken windows are boarded.
> The bronze weathervane cod has lost half its scales.
> The airy tanks are dry.
>
> Once my nose crawled like a snail on the glass;
> my hand tingled
> to burst the bubbles
> drifting from the noses of the cowed, compliant fish.

(SP 135)

Lowell takes us back to the territory of his childhood and, surrounded by the terror of the new, explodes the resonance of the old. Seeing the Aquarium in its state of disuse and neglect, prior to its destruction, brings back an intense and visually acute memory from his childhood, as though he were reenacting it, "Once my nose crawled like a snail on the glass." "The old South Boston Aquarium" was once an oasis, now its "airy tanks are dry." It was an oasis of sorts, but Lowell fixates on the most grotesque aspect of the fish in captivity: cowed, compliant.

Then, without warning, in an involuntary gesture:

> My hand draws back . . .

Lowell loses himself in time for a moment, and in the split second when this memory trace crosses the screen of consciousness, he feels as if he could reach through that chink into the other world; it is visibly, physically, there. His hand draws him back into the present where he reflects on his childhood and how often he wishes he were back there, a young boy in an old Aquarium, and he feels sad for his lost youth.

> We have to understand that the world can only be grasped by action, not by contemplation. The hand is more important than the eye . . . it is the hand that drives the subsequent evolution of the brain.[10]

Consider the implications of this for Lowell, whose first poem in *Lord Weary's Castle* ends with "your life is in your hands," and whose last poem in *Selected Poems*, "Dolphin," ends, "this book, half fiction,/ an eelnet made by man for the eel fighting— // *my eyes have seen what my hand did*" (*SP* 246, italics mine.) Two eyes, one hand. I've thought about this in terms of acceptance of responsibility for actions, no matter how repugnant to the conscience. "My hand tingled/ to burst the bubbles/ drifting from the noses of the cowed, compliant fish." "My hand draws back." Everywhere his hand ("this living hand") tells him what he's doing after he's done it. He hurls himself into an action and a dramatic situation and uses the poem as a way of exploring his own responses, seeing what's on his mind. Lowell acts first and asks questions later.

> My hand draws back. I often sigh still
> for the dark downward and vegetating kingdom
> of the fish and reptile. . . .
>
> (SP 135)

And now a new fence, itself horned and armored, is there to keep him out of his "Boston Common."

Though the poem is passionate and engaged, the title sets it in an ironic light. History used to be the living past: monuments marked moments of a past time *in* space, and the St. Gaudens' relief brings the event it commemorates to life so vividly "William James could almost hear the bronze Negroes breathe."

The poet's perception of the world has changed from the eagerness and the pleasure of going to the Aquarium and the basic comfort of being a child, pressing his nose right up to the glass, to the sadness of the adult standing behind the "barbed and galvanized// fence." Both the fence and the fish tanks of the Aquarium are barriers, impeding movement, encouraging him to stop and reflect. The child sees the fish as "cowed, compliant," which they're not, just as the world is not a safe place. And where he sees the Aquarium as an instance of neglect he sees the "barbed and galvanized// fence" as an active threat. And the Statehouse, sexually charged, "tingling," has let the excavations proceed—in the name of progress. The monument, too, is in the hands of the machines—real and political.

> Behind their cage,
> yellow dinosaur steamshovels were grunting
> as they cropped up tons of mush and grass
> to gouge their underworld garage.

These cowardly (yellow) dinosaurs, creatures of the "underworld garage" are prehistoric, brutal, and the fence that surrounds them is armored, horned—reptilian. The Republic that once housed "cowed, compliant fish," is now overrun by the "savage servility" it fostered.

All this presses on the poet's mind to bring the monument to life. He needs to imagine his way out of the present violent, deathly, and frightening scene, where the very ground underfoot is trembling, and there is no one to stop it. "Giant finned cars nose forward like fish." The people want an underground garage. They mean business. The Statehouse could fall apart without them even noticing. And all in the name of progress. Lowell seems to be saying that the idea of what constitutes necessity needs to be reevaluated. This is the social equivalent of Wittgenstein's comment on the state of philosophy: "We find certain things about seeing puzzling, because we do not find the whole business of seeing puzzling enough." It doesn't matter whether the mode of discourse is poetry or prose: it is a matter of illumination.

There is some wonder that America has survived its own history thus far, and a sense that its best, most humane and adventurous years are over. The reason that we feel the destruction of the Aquarium and the perilous place of the St. Gaudens' relief so intensely is that Lowell takes it so personally: it's as though it were being done to him. When he says, "Their monument sticks like a fishbone/ in the city's throat," we feel that fishbone catch in his throat.

The Boston Common, which occupies the center of Boston and the center of the poem, has become the symbolic center of America. The monument to the Civil War regiment is linked to Lowell's immediate concern for Civil Rights. It is racism that "sticks like a fishbone/ in the city's throat." The brutality of the modern machinery whose excavations are endangering the monument reflects a culture that is only interested in change of a mechanistic, technological sort—not the kind of humane qualitative change that would aid Civil Rights. America has changed from New England's Puritan spirit of "sparse, sincere rebellion" to a country of "giant finned cars"; its spirit is vanishing; it is better at gouging out underground garages than resolving its racial conflict.

The poet has arrived, through a series of observations and flashbacks, at the monument and Colonel Shaw and through him, or his image represented by St. Gaudens, finds an image of freedom.

> Its Colonel is as lean
> as a compass-needle.
>
> He has an angry wrenlike vigilance,
> a greyhound's gentle tautness;
> he seems to wince at pleasure,
> and suffocate for privacy.
>
> He is out of bounds now. He rejoices in man's lovely,
> peculiar power to choose life and die—
> when he leads his black soldiers to death,
> he cannot bend his back.

This young man, who had courage, toughness, and integrity, who "rejoices in man's lovely,/ peculiar power to choose life and die," has made a choice. He is relentless; "he cannot bend his back." If he does, he would collapse under the strain; "riding on his bubble,/ he waits/ for the blessèd break." In him, Lowell has found a viable hero. During his meditation in front of the statue the poet has already cemented his identification with Robert Gould Shaw.

The poem moves from the image of the dry Aquarium to the yellow steamshovels that have replaced both it and the St. Gaudens' monument as artifacts to be looked at, and on to a major statement about history and the future (and, in some ways, the impossibility of a future)—to the image of an image, the photograph of

> Hiroshima boiling
>
> over a Mosler Safe, the "Rock of Ages"
> that survived the blast. . . .

The Aquarium and the Statehouse have their counterparts in the garage, the steamshovels, and the Mosler Safe. Everything Lowell values is in immediate danger of disappearing. Lowell was well aware of the risk involved in writing a poem on a grand theme: "Nothing is easier than to take a heroic subject and get something paralyzed as a result" (*LCR*). Many people had written about Shaw before, including William Vaughn Moody and James Russell Lowell. William James, who was at the statue's dedication, finds his way into the poem through a quote from one of his letters which Elizabeth Hardwick had just been editing.

The moment of nostalgia wanes and is counteracted by a description of other—less individual—monuments to the Civil War:

> The stone statues of the abstract Union Soldier
> grow slimmer and younger each year—
> wasp-waisted, they doze over muskets
> and muse through their sideburns. . . .

It is possible that this stanza saves the poem from becoming topheavy—a victim of its own "heroic subject"—through this injection of humor, brought out by the marked contrast between himself growing older and thick-waisted in time, and the musket-bearing stone statues which seem to him to oppose time. He plays on the delusions of the conscious mind, the way in which, as we get older, suddenly everyone looks younger (and the old less ancient). It reminds me of the passage in *The Past Recaptured* when Marcel receives a letter signed "Your young friend" from someone he thought of as a peer. And it is his recognition that he is aging like the others he observes with horror—that time hasn't miraculously passed him by while devouring the lives of others—that gives him the necessary pressure to jolt him into action, which for him and Lowell means *writing*. Time is suspended only in the unconscious and it takes these external events to burst the bubble that envelops the self.

"For the Union Dead" encompasses an incredible regression. We will reach the moon before we learn what it is to be human. "Space is nearer./ When I crouch to my television set,/ the drained faces of Negro school-children rise like balloons." The balloons are a technological extension of the bubbles in the Aquarium and Lowell sees Shaw riding, not on his horse, but on the bubble that has risen from "the drained faces of the Negro school-children." Notice that this sequence of associations is not only held together by the Civil War / Civil Rights issue of racial freedom, but also by the visual shift in shape of the bubble-to-balloon-to-bubble image and by the time shift from Lowell's own childhood, to Shaw's youth, to the Negro school-children.

Nothing could be more tenuous than the image of Shaw "riding on his bubble"—caught between extinction and change. The poem takes place at a moment in history when something positive could happen: the situation of the Negro school-children has made the news. But Lowell hasn't much hope of that.

> The Aquarium is gone. Everywhere,
> giant finned cars nose forward like fish;
> a savage servility
> slides by on grease.

When the poet moves away from Shaw to say, "The ditch is nearer," a line that could serve as a subtitle for the book, we sense extinction encroaching on the individual, the state, and the globe. The poem which began with a longing for the sea—"the dark downward and vegetating kingdom/ of the fish and reptile"—ends on a negative epiphany, with harsh sibilants hissing. The inhuman has come to dominate and the poem ends on a note of impotence and disgust, with the depletion and annihilation of the natural order.

In *Life Studies* Lowell mastered the variable free verse line, and this mastery allowed him to set his kind of dramatic-narrative-lyric into quatrains which in turn allowed him a freedom from linear time. In "For the Union Dead" ten stanzas take place in the present and seven in the past. This is a much more complex and sophisticated shifting of present and past tense than we have heretofore seen in Lowell's work. "Memories of West Street and Lepke," for example, begins in the present with observations of the locale, and then leaps into a singular, isolated image from his past which he lets unfold. In "For the Union Dead" the quatrains are in sharp contrast to the occasion. The more formless the situation, the more Lowell tries to give it form. Here the quatrains contain the stop and start of the gait and link the poem to history, setting up a dialogue, a dialectic, a duel, between the old and the new, decay versus renovation. And the structure of remembrance, the innate tyranny of memory, turns into a distillation of pain. Lowell reiterates Proust's insight that the force that circles the earth the most number of times in a second is not electricity but pain. What makes Lowell's later poetry so moving is that the struggle takes place in the light of day: things have names and named things have a history; objects can be tracked to their sources; moral actions are possible, like leaps of faith, like Pascal's wager, like Colonel Shaw's decision to "choose life and die."

How sour the knowledge travellers bring away!
The world's monotonous and small; we see
ourselves today, tomorrow, yesterday,
an oasis of horror in sands of ennui!

Shall we move or rest? Rest, if you can rest;
move if you must. One runs, but others drop
and trick their vigilant antagonist.
Time is a runner who can never stop.

("The Voyage," *I* 71; Baudelaire: *Le voyage*.)

CHAPTER 4

Words Meat-Hooked

from the Living Steer

He admitted but four elementary principles, or more strictly, conditions, of bliss. That which he considered chief was (strange to say!) the simple and purely physical one of free exercise in the open air. . . . His second condition was the love of woman. His third, and most difficult of realization, was the contempt of ambition. His fourth was an object of unceasing pursuit; and he held that, other things being equal, the extent of attainable happiness was in proportion to the spirituality of this object.

—Poe

So much life and never!
So many years and always my weeks!
—Vallejo

During the ten years between *Near the Ocean* and *Day by Day*, Lowell wrote hundreds of fourteen-line, unrhymed iambic pentameter poems—his adaptation of the sonnet. These were published in a series of volumes—*Notebook* (1969), *Notebook* (1970), *History, For Lizzie and Harriet*, and *The Dolphin*, the last three published in 1973. *Notebook* (1970) is a revised and expanded version of the earlier *Notebook*, which Lowell quarried into *History* and *For Lizzie and Harriet*. The former, as the title suggests, includes the poems on historical themes. The latter contains love poems and "letters" to, from, and about his wife and daughter, which stirred up much indignation among poets and reviewers, who criticized him for overstepping the boundaries between life and art. *The Dolphin* charts a year, from summer to summer. The plot, such as it is, revolves around the breakup with his wife, Elizabeth Hardwick, and his relationship with Caroline Blackwood. Replete with images of marine life, it is as if the salmon in "Waking Early Sunday Morning" had broken loose and been transformed into the playful, erotic dolphin, symbol of his muse.

> Any clear thing that blinds us with surprise,
> your wandering silences and bright trouvailles,
> dolphin let loose to catch the flashing fish. . . .
>
> ("Fishnet," *SP* 227)

Rarely have the concerns of high art and topicality come together so forcibly. The *Notebook* project is unified by the sonnet form and the final effect is that personal and public history are equalized. My concern in this chapter is with this overall project, rather than with the way Lowell chose to revise and reorder the appearance of the poems in the successive volumes. As before, the main text is *Selected Poems*, which contains 143 of the sonnets, many of the best of his fourteen-liners.

The importance of this project to his oeuvre is, in the main, an unaddressed question. Some of his staunchest followers have had difficulty coming to terms with it. The sheer bulk of the work, with all of its revisions, may be overwhelming, but Lowell is careful to define his terms. In "The Nihilist as Hero" he sets down a new aesthetic credo: "I want words meat-hooked from the living steer" (*SP*, 183). And he has an argument relative to history which he puts forth in "History": "History has to live with what was here" (*SP*, 159).

There's a case to be made that *Notebook* and its successors, taken as a whole, constitute Lowell's grandest scheme. The project is a modern epic amalgamating Berryman's form for *The Dream Songs*—a long poem made up of discrete short poems, each eighteen lines long, connected through the voice of the narrator rather than the narrative—and Pound's method of historical collage in *The Cantos*—his way of layering the text with significant allusions. Lowell remarked to Stanley Kunitz,

> The modern poem of length that interests me most . . . is Pound's Cantos, the only long poem of the century that really comes off, even with all its flaws.[1]

And the description of Berryman's poem in Lowell's review of *77 Dream Songs* looks forward to his own practice in *Notebook:*

> His [Berryman's] writing has been a long, often back-breaking search for an inclusive style, a style that could use his erudition, and catch the high, even frenetic, intensity of his experiences. . . . By their impertinent piety, by jumping from thought to thought, mood to mood, and by saying anything that comes into the author's head, they are touching and nervously alive.[2]

Lowell goes on to say that it was the fixed form, each in three stanzas, that enabled Berryman to say anything that came into his head. Lowell fastened on the fixed boundaries of the fourteen-liner to give himself the same freedom.

I sense, too, that another model for Lowell's particular kind of layered, hybrid, triadic form is to be found in Keats, the precursor of the modernity we ascribe to Rimbaud. I can't conceive of *Notebook* without the precedent of "On First Looking into Chapman's Homer," "On Seeing the Elgin Marbles," or "On Sitting Down to Read 'King Lear' Again"—poems whose triggering subjects are books and artifacts, springboards for internal voyages. If Lowell learned about narrative and how to make ordinary detail carry symbolic weight from Tolstoy, he learned from Keats how to leap from crag to crag and travel vast distances in fourteen lines. The structure, as a whole, was particularly congenial to Lowell's temperament.

> But we cannot go back to Charles V
> barreled in armor, more gold fleece than king;
> he haws on the gristle of a Flemish word,
> · his upper and lower Hapsburg jaws won't meet.
> The sunset he tilts at is big Venetian stuff,
> the true Charles, done by Titian, never lived.
> The battle he rides offstage to is offstage.
>
> ("Charles V by Titian," *SP* 168)

The *Notebook* poems are difficult to read consecutively but merit close attention. They offer many of the hazards and rewards of Blake's prophetic books in that not all of the material has been assimilated into art and yet the urgency, dynamism, and incisiveness of such impossible projects is commensurate with the task.

Lowell puts forth his intentions for the *Notebook* project in this brief description from the interview in *Modern Occasions:*

> *Notebook* mixes the day-to-day with the history—the lamp by a tree out this window on Redcliff Square . . . or maybe the rain, but always the instant, sometimes changing to the lost. A flash of haiku to lighten the distance. Has this something to do with a rhymeless sonnet? One poem must lead towards the next, but is fairly complete; it can stride on stilts, or talk.[3]

The poems are like collages, joining disparate, seemingly disconnected things: the nature of the day, something in the news, something out of history, the condition of the speaker. These can appear in any order, and they give the poems a fierce, syllogistic effect. He stops time just long enough to let space, color, weather, landscape, texture filter in before they all dissolve in the final fade-out, assertion, or denial. He seems fruitfully torn between the particular and the general, and if the poems don't match up to his more finished products, they do carry on a similar dialogue between thought and action.

It is passionate speech he desires. He must explain himself to others, appease the gods, expunge his bottomless guilt: "We stand and hear the pummeling unpurged" ("Window," *SP*, 227). It is the speech of the man who broods, who scrutinizes existence: the man who seeks to find meaning in his own ups and downs. The self finds itself everywhere; Lowell can locate a whole life-cycle in a given mood swing.

SYMPTOMS

I fear my conscience because it makes me lie.
A dog seems to lap water from the pipes,
life-enhancing water brims my bath—
(the bag of waters or the lake of the grave . . . ?)
from the palms of my feet to my wet neck—
I have no mother to lift me in her arms.
I feel my old infection, it comes once yearly:
lowered good humor, then an ominous
rise of irritable enthusiasm. . . .
Three dolphins bear our little toilet-stand,
the grin of the eyes rebukes the scowl of the lips,
they are crazy with the thirst. I soak,
examining and then examining
what I really have against myself.

(*SP* 228)

Lowell's best sonnets, such as this one, are extended synapses. And the gravity and stateliness of the language and intention are counterpointed by the lowliness and absurdity of the situation of the man in the bathtub.

Complaint breeds invention. Lowell's sonnets have a rending brevity because he wants to test his ideas or propositions poetically, against experience, and taking nothing for granted, he prods his questing, questioning spirit further. He is suspicious of all labels, all fixed categories and habits of mind, and often takes an otherworldly view of this world writing with an eye to the impossible, seeing everything as connected and constantly changing—"Life by definition breeds on change" ("The Nihilist as Hero," *SP* 183)—and our capacity to posit alternative realities as part of what changes reality itself.

What these poems lack in length they make up for in duration. They make me think of a series of mental flashes as fireworks flaring and staying in the air, taking hold of the air, rather than dying, so that layer upon layer is transposed and nothing is lost. Sometimes I don't know whether he's trying to hit the center of the target, the tree behind the subject, or the apple on the subject's head.

These "rhymeless sonnets," like his longer poems "For the Union Dead" and "Waking Early Sunday Morning," work to incorporate randomness into a structure that appears inevitable, not provisional. Poems composed of fragmentary perceptions are not themselves necessarily fragments. A poem may need a triggering subject but it doesn't have to be overtly mentioned. The "I"/"Thou" relationship, the preverbal dynamic, can be hidden in many ways.

Commenting on *Notebook* (1970) in an "Afterthought," Lowell says:

> As the title intends, the poems in this book are written as one poem, intuitive in arrangement, but not a pile or sequence of related material. It is less an almanac than the story of my life . . . I began working sometime in June 1967 and finished in June 1970. My plot rolls with the seasons, but one year is confused with another. I have flashbacks to what I remember, and fables inspired by impulse. Accident threw up subjects, and the plot swallowed them—famished for human chances.

.   .   .

I lean heavily to the rational, but am devoted to unrealism. . . .
Unrealism can degenerate into meaningless clinical hallucinations
or rhetorical machinery, but the true unreal is about something,
and eats from the abundance of reality.

                                                        (*N* 262)

Lowell's interest in the *provisional* allowed him to sift for
poetry, for what René Char called "bits of incorruptible being
snatched from the repugnant jaws of death." Sift for poetry? I
mean submit to chance. Get away from the poetry of heightened, significant, epiphanic moments. His use and exploration
of the sonnet for these poems is identical to his use of other
forms at other times in his life: a form to roam in, a magnet to
catch his associations, salvage his fleeting thoughts and keep his
daily output within his visible control. Hopkins confessed he
might not have written his late work at all had it not been for
the fixed boundaries and rigidity of the sonnet.

The sonnet is also an historical choice. The form itself is
not a neutral thing. "My meter, fourteen line unrhymed blank
verse sections, is fairly strict at first and elsewhere, but often
corrupts in single lines to the freedom of prose. Even with this
license, I fear I have failed to avoid the themes and gigantism of
the sonnet" ("Afterthought," *N* 263).

❧❧❧

All of Lowell's concerns make their appearance in the *Notebook* sonnets. Especially history, his ongoing obsession. And what
did Lowell mean by "history" when he invoked the word or
called in sequence of *Notebook* sonnets *History*, a title that is more
arrogant but less audacious than *The Cantos?* "What is history?
What you cannot touch," he tells us in "Mexico (4)" (*SP* 202).

Not all thoughts can find adequate expression or form within a given era. Each generation of poets inherits certain myths, some of which they explore, some of which they explode to make room for new ones. Some myths liberate the imagination; others stifle it. In our time history has become myth or its equivalent in terms of imaginative action and Lowell treats it as such. He was born too late to view history as exotic, like Pound or Eliot, and too early to mistrust its construction. Now, we all live *in* the thought of vanishing, having seen so many actual things go, be replaced. We have witnessed everything of late go forward in reverse; terms like *radical, underground, progressive, avant-garde,* mean the opposite of what they used to mean or less than what they meant (as little as fifteen years ago) and embody phenomenally easy conservatisms. The same dilution pertains to literary terms—like "free verse" or "stream of consciousness." History is a human form of consolation, e.g., if that—place or action—*was,* then history, which hinges on the future tense, *will be.* It is a system of belief that branches out through *isms,* which vary the theme. I speak, as a man of my time, in the hope that what I perceive to be true will change and change in specific directions.

꽃

Lowell's way with history is purely dialectical. He probes his own perceptions, the conflict and confluence between moments in time,

> Summer hail flings crystals on the window—
> they wrapped Lady Ann's head in a white handkerchief. . . .
> ("Death of Anne Boleyn," *SP* 167)

Today leads to yesterday and yesterday to today. Yesterday encompasses the total past, from the previous moment to prehistory. Everything we perceive, by the time we recognize it, is by definition past; therefore, all history is now—we experience the past in the present. It is easier in theory than in practice to accept the idea that the perceiver alters the nature of the thing perceived. Lowell's exploration of the ramifications of this notion culminates in *Notebook*. By the time he writes these poems he has begun to see *everything* as history, with himself in the role of necessarily unreliable narrator. This is the premise that underlies *History* and the poem "History."

HISTORY

History has to live with what was here,
clutching and close to fumbling all we had—
it is so dull and gruesome how we die,
unlike writing, life never finishes.
Abel was finished; death is not remote,
a flash-in-the-pan electrifies the skeptic,
his cows crowding like skulls against high-voltage wire,
his baby crying all night like a new machine.
As in our Bibles, white-faced, predatory,
the beautiful, mist-drunken hunter's moon ascends—
a child could give it a face: two holes, two holes,
my eyes, my mouth, between them a skull's no-nose—
O there's a terrifying innocence in my face
drenched with the silver salvage of the mornfrost.

(*SP* 159)

The phrase "History has to live with what was here," though tautological, is not self-evident. Lowell wants us to take this assertion at face value. I can think of few absolutes that are as straightforward, intriguing, and in the end mysterious, as this one.

Putting his poetic intensions momentarily to the side, I want to investigate this use and view of history. Doesn't Lowell have it backwards: isn't *history* "what was here," and aren't we the ones who have to live with it? Or, if history is "what you cannot touch," and if "what was here" is not history, then what is it

history has to live with? Everything that has occurred that cannot be erased? Events, or myths, acts or thoughts? Is history a
continually active force forced into a passive condition insofar as
it "has to live with what was here"? Or is this like Faulkner's
spokesman, Gavin Stevens, the lawyer in *Intruder in the Dust*,
who, stunned by the repetition of old events in new guises, and
the tragic way fate hounds a man, says: "The past isn't past. It's
not even past."

Lowell knew that the moment you begin to question an
object (of consciousness) you change it. For him, as for Elizabeth Bishop, knowledge was "historical, flowing, and flown."[4]
It is as if he had asked himself, "What is history? What if I
throw everything that 'was here' into the same vat and equalize
it within the domain of consciousness?" Lowell experimented
with the idea of questioning accepted truths. He questioned all
our basic assumptions, received ideas. He wrote *History* in dis-
trust of philosophy because philosophy doesn't answer to the
ceaseless barrage of information that assaults us from all parts of
the world—turning the world into a global village which houses
its archives in an infinite storage comparment, a sieve with a
trap door. And this clear, open-ended idea about history opened
up a host of possibilities.

> History has to live with what was here,

Like husbands and wives. Nothing is forgotten, but the pattern
recurs, each time defining itself through its *signs:*

> clutching and close to fumbling all we had—

in this instance, football—the modern gladiator sport; and history—the player who is holding the ball. The crowd's eyes are
on him at this instant and he knows that he will have to fall
momentarily—be crucially, brutally tackled—and that, beyond
doing his best to gain yards—make progress—the one thing he

mustn't do is fumble, let go of the ball. In another poem, "Long Summers (*Months of it*)" (*SP* 191), the runner is buried "on the cleated field" because he would not let go of the ball; that player would rather die than relinquish it.

"Close to fumbling"—Lowell has prepared us for this state-ment in previous religious and historical poems (from "The Quaker Graveyard in Nantucket" to "For the Union Dead") that meditate on the possibility of extinction.

A daunting beginning. It makes me want to listen. And then—don't we all know that death is "dull and gruesome"? It's not; it's all in "*how* we die" (italics mine). And what does he mean by "life never finishes"? One way of reading this line is that "unlike writing," which may be a session of writing that begins at 7 and ends at 10 or may be an art-work written in time (a poem is finished, a story finishes—it has an end), "life never finishes," which could mean simply that it keeps going on, there's always something else, it's never over, as perceived by someone who's living, moment to moment. But, considered from another angle, Lowell has shrewdly reversed Horace's adage: *Ars longa, vita brevis*. "Life never finishes"; it ends. And most of us have the art/life problem backwards if "unlike writing, life never fin-ishes."

The first movement has ended. Four lines and all this knotty complication? I would have to read "unlike writing, life never finishes" as an aphorism. The first line of the poem lends itself to such a treatment, the fourth doesn't. I think of Gide, who asked his readers not to read him too quickly, as I leap ahead to the next line.

> Abel was finished; death is not remote,

"Abel was finished." The *Bible* was written, Abel's story was told, completed, his "death is not remote"; he survives as myth in history. Before Cain killed Abel, men killed creatures in order to survive. Cain initiated murder: man's second fall. Cain changed death's paradigms. Psychological motives meld with the babble of tongues. And "Abel" was also "finished," as equal to "was murdered" as in "Let's finish that guy off. . ."

> a flash-in-the-pan electrifies the skeptic,
> his cows crowding like skulls against high-voltage wire,
> his baby crying all night like a new machine.

These lines remind me of poems in "Life Studies" with their images of the electric chair and shock treatment. The leap from "life never finishes" to "a flash-in-the-pan" makes us stop and wonder. Has loss of faith in God been replaced by the mechanical? Has superficial shock replaced inner revelation? It doesn't take much—"a flash-in-the-pan"—for this "skeptic" to renounce his lack of faith; and the moment he does, he loses his humanity. Where he might have seen life, he sees death. Is this what enlightenment has led to?

There's a science fiction element in this passage I hadn't noticed before in Lowell's work: the last two lines grow more gruesome the longer you look at them—the cows sizzle—and Lowell's skeptic is so far removed from his own emotions, his baby's cries mean nothing, they merely *jar*.

> As in our Bibles, white-faced, predatory,
> the beautiful, mist-drunken hunter's moon ascends—
> a child could give it a face: two holes, two holes,
> my eyes, my mouth, between them a skull's no-nose—

Notice how the moon has been instantiated and supplanted at the same time. This is an instance of the way Lowell's work goes far beyond the realms of subject matter into the caverns of emotion and the canyons of language. The poem succeeds through more than mere conviction of voice: it has the commitment of a life behind its turnings.

That phrase "a child could give it a face" is the most unexpected moment in the poem. The child is a hopeful being. It has imagination and innocence, freshness. Lowell's "moon" is encrusted by his associations, literary and mythical. It is unusual, even for him, to surround one noun with this many—four—adjectives.

Lowell is lyrical in the most unlikely places. Something extraordinary happens after the "mist-drunken hunter's moon ascends"—and in plain, transparent language. The child points to another way of seeing and being and fills up the blankness of matter with emptiness, just to please itself: "two holes, two holes," embodying purity and savagery in the self-satisfaction of natural desire—unlike the corruption of values alluded to earlier. This leads the narrator out of his lair. The child's notion of a face is highly abstract. The same blankness of matter terrifies the narrator, who sees his own eyes and mouth and "between them a skull's no-nose," death's head and self-portrait up there. Why? Because his hold on reality is so tenuous he needs to see himself reflected in order to convince himself that he exists. The child's directive helps him to begin again. "Terrifying innocence" is what he needs to go on.

All in all, Lowell's "History" is less forbidding when read in conjunction with this sentence by Heraclitus, as translated by Guy Davenport: "History is a child building a sand-castle by the sea, and that child is the whole majesty of man's power in the world."[5]

❦

History, like *The Cantos*, sends the reader on an endless search for sources. It is impossible to know when a passage derives significantly from a previous text unless we happen to have read the source. A case in point is "Long Summers (Two in the

Afternoon)." No one could have known at the time that the first
half of the poem is essentially an imitation of a poem by Osip
Mandelstam (sometimes called "Insomnia") to which Lowell
probably had access through Olga Carlisle, with whom he had
worked on other Mandelstam translations for the anthology, *Poets
on Street Corners*.

LONG SUMMERS

Two in the afternoon. The restlessness.
Greek Islands. Maine. I have counted the catalogue
of ships down half its length: the blistered canvas,
the metal bowsprits, once pricking up above
the Asian outworks like a wedge of geese,
the migrant yachtsmen, and the fleet in irons . . . .
The iron bell is rocking like a baby,
the high tide's turning on its back exhausted,
the colored, dreaming, silken spinnakers
shove through the patches in the island pine,
as if vegetating millennia of lizards fed
on fern and cropped the treetops . . . a nation of gazelles,
straw-chewers in the African siesta . . . .
I never thought scorn of things; struck fear in no man.

(*SP* 192)

NO. 78

Insomnia. Homer. Taut sails.
I've read to the middle of the catalogue of ships,
that long litter, that train of cranes,
that once set forth above Hellas.

Where are you sailing like a wedge of cranes
into alien zones, a godly foam
on your leaders' heads? Helen gone, Achaian men,
what would Troy alone be worth to you?

The sea and Homer both—all moves by force of love.
Whom should I listen to? Even Homer's silent now,
and now the dark sea roars rhetorically
its billowy thunder above my pillowed head.[6]

Mandelstam's poem has a lyric integrity, a purity not sought after by Lowell.

Homer's world is lost to Mandelstam and Mandelstam's world is lost to Lowell. Lowell is as far away from Mandelstam in tone as he is from Keats; they both work through the materials of the imagined scene toward climax and satisfaction; whereas, Lowell tests one connection after another, hesitates twice—which accounts for the use of ellipses in successive lines, and ends on a note of grave, outrageous irony, "I never thought scorn of things; struck fear in no man."

Where Mandelstam counts the catalogue of ships to put himself to sleep, Lowell uses it to give his restlessness direction. Midway through the poem, Lowell moves away from his sources, Mandelstam and Homer, and looks down at the harbor in Castine, Maine, where the boats are moored. He seems to want to conjure peace—and does at the end. But before that he sees, in the "Asian outworks," a reminder of the Vietnam War, which was at its peak, and why the "fleet" is "in irons."

The way to explain the shifts in tone in this and other poems written between 1965 and 1970 is through the Vietnam War, and its omnipresence in the media as a visual event. We can't help but associate America girding up its loins for battle with Homer's list of ships before the sack of Troy. The high tide's exhaustion is not Lowell's—it's America's—and Lowell has felt it before in another war:

> Let the sea-gulls wail
>
> For water, for the deep where the high tide
> Mutters to its hurt self, mutters and ebbs.
> ("The Quaker Graveyard in Nantucket," *SP* 8)

In "Long Summers," Lowell sees the future as an "iron bell," and implies that in order to survive we will have to make ourselves harder, more armored, reptilian. This meditation has become so painful that his mind transforms the pain and suddenly the poem becomes a beautiful reverie on the old America, which is still to some extent present, if endangered. He sees the sails, "the colored, dreaming, silken spinnakers," passing behind "the patches in the island pine," and his imagination dissolves the mechanistic aspects of the scene, "the fleet in irons . . ./ The iron bell," in the scene at the harbor. He finds his way to pre-history and primitive innocence, "vegetating millennia of liz-ards." This shift occurs when he sees the sails "shove through the patches in the island pine,/ *as if*" (my emphasis) they were prehistoric creatures, which changes his reverie into a vivid fan-tasy, a wish for the return to a peaceful world, "a nation of gazelles," most graceful and swift of all animals! And his choice of the gazelle is not merely visually accurate or poetically right, it is hinged to his deeper longings.

Keats and Mandelstam stay inside the imagination, they reign in distances that exist in time, not space, and transform them respectively into image—"Silent, upon a peak in Dar-ien"—and sound—"and now the dark sea roars rhetorically/ its billowy thunder above my pillowed head." The ego, embedded in the scene, dissolves, is everywhere present and nowhere visi-ble as a thing-in-itself. In Lowell's poems the self is the pivot. There is always his romantic, mythic self moving through his words.

Lowell felt confined by his personal history and thought of history itself as a hiatus from his premature entombment. But he could never write himself out of time into any kind of time-less realm. He could, however, give the reader the feeling of what it was like to be alive at a given moment: his speech, in his later work, is under the pressure of a moment that will not re-cur.

In a minute, two inches of rain stream through my dry
garden stones, clear as crystal, without trout—
we have gone down and down, gone the wrong brook.

("Bosworth Field," SP 166)

These later poems, especially, are all about this; they take
on the perilous instant. Before the sonnets, this particular thread
is more concealed by art, but accounts perhaps for the specificity and uniqueness he tried to give every object, every action.

I watch a feverish huddle of shivering cows;
you sit making a fishspine from a chestnut leaf.

("Fall Weekend at Milgate," I, SP 231)

※※

The bloody massacre in Bangladesh quickly covered over the
memory of the Russian invasion of Czechoslovakia, the assassi-
nation of Allende drowned out the groans of Bangladesh, the war
in the Sinai Desert made people forget Allende, the Cambodian
massacre made people forget Sinai, and so on and so forth until
ultimately everyone lets everything be forgotten.

In times when history still moved slowly, events were few and
far between and easily committed to memory. They formed a
commonly accepted *backdrop* for thrilling scenes of adventure in
private life. Nowadays, history moves at a brisk clip. A historical
event, though soon forgotten, sparkles the morning after with the
dew of novelty. No longer a backdrop, it is now the *adventure*
itself, an adventure enacted before the backdrop of the commonly
accepted banality of private life.[7]

Not all of Lowell's best sonnets are included in *Selected Poems*.
"Che Guevara" is the first of a six-part sequence in *Notebook* with
the catch-all seasonal title, "October and November," referring

to the months in 1967 when the poems were written and not the intrinsic quality of the season, late fall, autumn. The poem illustrates how Lowell combined, and in this case fortuitously merged, topicality and history. Guevara is the kind of man for whom Lowell had searched in the past: a man who stood for something, like freedom, and, like Robert Gould Shaw, chose to "choose life and die."

> CHE GUEVARA
>
> Week of Che Guevara, hunted, hurt,
> held prisoner one lost day, then gangstered down
> for gold, for justice—violence cracking on violence,
> rock on rock, the corpse of the last armed prophet
> laid out on a sink in a shed, revealed by flashlight—
> as the leaves light up, still green, this afternoon,
> and burn to frittered reds; as the oak, branch-lopped
> to go on living, swells with goiters like a fruit-tree,
> as the sides of the high white stone buildings over-
> shadow the poor, too new in the new world,
> Manhattan, where our clasped, illicit hands
> pulse, stop the bloodstream as if it hit rock. . . .
> Rest for the outlaw . . . kings once hid in oaks,
> with prices on their heads, and watched for game.
>
> *(N 53)*

But the crucial difference between Guevara and Shaw for Lowell was that Guevara was a contemporary, and Lowell didn't have time to assimilate the ultimate meaning of his life and death. He was too involved in it for that. Isn't this how modern man keeps time, through the news? Lowell marks time through the news of Guevara's eventual capture and death. Guevara's death brought Lowell to his senses and heightened the moment he was living in.

The phrasing of the first line starts off more urgently than many of Lowell's *Notebook* entries, more like an ordinary notebook. "*Week of* Che Guevara. . . ." Lowell has been taken aback, stunned, consumed by this event and is still finding his way tentatively into his subject, "hunted, hurt," looking for an opening. Guevara was a symbol of hope for Lowell and like-minded people who thought the world could be changed for the good by his example. Guevara was the last world revolutionary, "the last armed prophet." After fighting in Cuba, helping Castro overthrow Batista, Guevara went on. Writing as well as fighting. While engaged in guerilla warfare deep in the Bolivian jungle where he was to die, Guevara's concerns were as much with the war in Vietnam as with the battle he was waging at the time. He never lost sight of the larger issues at hand: that his life— and death—were part of the means to an end. This helps explain Lowell's attraction to him and Lowell's humility when confronted with a subject whose integrity was inviolable. In an essay published in the *New Left Review* in 1967, "Vietnam Must Not Stand Alone," Guevara wrote:

> Wherever death may surprise us, let it be welcome, provided that this, our battle-cry, may have reached some receptive ear and another hand may be extended to wield our weapons and other men be ready to intone the funeral dirge with the staccato chant of the machine-gun and new battle-cries of war and victory.[8]

John Berger reported in his essay entitled " 'Che' Guevara": "At the news of Guevara's death, I heard someone say: 'He was the world symbol of the possibilities of one man.' Why is this true? Because he recognized what was intolerable for man and acted accordingly."[9] "What was intolerable for man" was the springboard of Lowell's poetry all along, the source of the rage that would never let go of him, of the wail, the outcry against the inhuman nature, of the human condition that kept him singing to stay alive, fighting the terrible perimeters of his own fate, and madness. The Irish poet and critic Seamus Heaney confronts this particular aspect of Lowell's character when he writes:

"Lowell's bravery was different from the bravery of John Berryman or Sylvia Plath, with whom his name has often been joined. They swam away powerfully into the dark swirls of the unconscious and the drift towards death, but Lowell resisted that, held fast to conscience and pushed deliberately towards self-mastery."[10]

Lowell was doing his best, in his life as well as his work, to oppose the war in Vietnam, and yet his gestures, such as refusing Lyndon Johnson's invitation to a White House party for artists, or joining in the march on the Pentagon, contained none of the risk that constituted the basis of Guevara's life. Lowell's risks were as a poet—the language he used and the subject matter he introduced. The newspaper photograph showed Guevara's body filled with bullet holes and burnt and his fingers had been lopped off. The use of the verb "gangstered" not only conveys the sleazy circumstances surrounding Guevara's brutal death and posthumous mutilation, it is also a peculiarly American concept, both in reality and myth. (And we know this is not the first appearance of the underworld in Lowell's poetry.) Our typical gangster uses a tommy gun and riddles his victim's body with bullets.

How many poets are willing and/or able to deal with such gritty material? Stevens could confront death matter-of-factly and say, "Death is absolute and without memorial,"[11] looking it right in the eye, but he never stained his imagined world with gangsters and when he writes about war he sounds like a minister lulling a half-empty congregation to sleep.

> How red the rose that is the soldier's wound,
> The wounds of many soldiers, the wounds of all
> The soldiers that have fallen, red in blood,
> The soldier of time grown deathless in great size.[12]

Guevara had a price on his head and was gunned down "for gold," with "justice" dragged in as part of the state's rhetoric. With these phrases Lowell shifts from the prosaic diction of the beginning, starts plying the language with "gangstered," and leaves us to fill in the visual details suggested by the sound of whips cracking and rifles firing in "violence cracking on violence,/ rock on rock"—a fine instance of the use of his auditory imagination.

The body "revealed by flashlight" is just *there*. Guevara, in Heidegger's terms, was "capable of death as death," something which Lowell is aware of and I think slightly overwhelmed by. Paraphrasing one of Wittgenstein's mystical aphorisms, he ends another fourteen-liner with the line, "Death's not an event in life, it's not lived through," ("Plotted," *SP* 236); and yet Guevara's death in some essential way countermands this statement.

The dash at the end of the fifth line signifies a shift in the poem. Lowell looks up from his desk just before sunset, stressing the present tense, "*this* afternoon," and no sooner has he lifted his eyes than the sun sets. One moment it's summer, the next it's fall: the leaves turn red and crumble. In one instant a season changes just as in one moment a man who was alive is dead. Lowell fantasized death all of his life, projected it in numerous manifestations, intended to ward off its reality. But the sudden onset of fall is coterminous with dying. "Frittered" is a key word here: it pertains to Guevara and Lowell, carries with it the pain of regret and finality and waste, and refers to the imperviousness of nature toward human activity, which Lowell sees as a kind of cosmic injustice.

Half way through the seventh line the poem makes another turning—the diction rises to the hieratic. I wonder if the lines referring to "the oak, branch-lopped/ to go on living" and swelling with "goiters" are meant to give a positive meaning to Guevara's death and, as a consequence, hope—hope for himself, for the poor, for all who were suffering what was intolerable for man. In a time when many poets split up words for trivial sound effect, Lowell, by breaking "over-/ shadow" the way he does, gives the word an authentic doubleness. On the one hand the poor are overshadowed, in shadow, and shadowed by the "high white stone buildings," the halls of money and justice which Lowell distrusts. On the other hand, "shadow" is an Americanism that pairs off with "gangstered." "To shadow" or "to put a shadow on a man" means, ominously, to follow someone without being noticed. Lowell regards the poor, "too new in the new world," with compassion.

"Manhattan," with the word framed, set off in a phrase, is where the poem makes a characteristically jarring connection back to Lowell and his own passionate love affair, and it is through these "clasped, illicit hands," and this "illicit" liaison that he feels himself connected to Guevara, whose fingers had been lopped off, as if he felt himself an "outlaw" in this implied adultery.

I don't know what he means at the end in his glance backward to another time with its gentle, nostalgic tone. Did the "kings" have it better in exile? He makes their "oaks" sound more like the Forest of Arden than the danger zones where deposed kings took refuge from a new regime. The phrase in the penultimate line, "Rest for the outlaw," seems to be a hymn, or a prayer, a quieter version of his outburst in the earlier poem "Florence" ("Pity the monsters!") in a world in which neither the poet nor the outlaw nor the "last armed prophet" can find rest or peace—even in death.

Lowell's historical sonnets are a lesson about history. He presses upon us the knowledge that we cannot see the past except through the lens of the present. Our vision is tinged by the time we are in. Purity is out of the question. It's not that essential truth doesn't exist—it just doesn't pertain. Contingency is all.

Lowell's approach toward history, which, though less profound than it has sometimes been ascribed to be, was always
wonderfully alive. He was consumed by the belief that history
is determined by the actions of great men, especially military
men. This is evidenced by his infatuation with Napoleon, the
quintessential military hero who was part of the nineteenth-cen-
tury literary tradition.

>   They loved the man of war,
> this small man with his hands behind his back,
> whose shadow, moving to and fro, was black
> behind the lighted tent. Still believing, they
> accused their destiny of *lese-majesté*.
> His misfortune had mounted on their back.
> The man of glory shook. Cold stupefied
> him, then suddenly he felt terrified.
> Being without belief, he turned to God:
> "God of armies, is this the end?" he cried.
> And then at last the expiation came,
> as he heard some one call him by his name,
> some one half-lost in shadow, who said, "No,
> Napoleon." Napoleon understood,
> restless, bareheaded, leaden, as he stood
> before his butchered legions in the snow.
>
>   ("Russia 1812," *I* 42–43;
>   Victor Hugo: *L'expiation*)

Julien Sorel in *The Red and the Black* modeled himself after Napoleon, and Raskolnikov in *Crime and Punishment* had a portrait
of him in his miserable, cramped garret room—Napoleon, the
Corsican colonel, that bold upstart who represented the victory
of the outsider in an age when there was always a "career open
to talent." Napoleon first appears in the nursery in "Commander

Lowell," where Robert's mother reads to him from "the Napoleon book." This Napoleon who "scratched his navel,/ and bolted
his food" represents the infantile root of the adult's attitude toward power and men of power. One could say he imbibed Napoleon at his mother's breast. Napoleon crops up throughout
Lowell's work. He even has a sonnet dedicated to him.

NAPOLEON

Boston's used bookshops, anachronisms from London,
are gone; it's hard to guess now why I spent
my vacations lugging home his third-hand *Lives*—
shaking the dust from that stationary stock:
cheap deluxe lithographs and gilt-edged pulp
on a man . . . not bloodthirsty, not sparing of blood,
with an eye and *sang-froid* to manage everything;
his iron hand no mere appendage of his mind
for improbable contingencies . . .
for uprooting races, lineages, Jacobins—
the price was paltry . . . three million soldiers dead,
grand opera fixed like morphine in their veins.
Dare we say, he had no moral center?
All gone like the smoke of his own artillery?

(*SP* 172)

This poem is followed by these lines in "Beethoven": "Beethoven was a Romantic, but too good;/ did kings, republics or
Napoleon teach him?/ He was his own Napoleon" (*SP* 173).

Lowell, the liberal and pacifist, perceived Napoleon as
someone who existed outside the sphere of any moral universe,
"not bloodthirsty, not sparing of blood,"—the blood of others
that is. Napoleon represents the spirit of separation, the heroic
achievement of one man who does things to achieve the approval
of others: a dead center that galvanizes action. Napoleon is just
one of a succession of generals and conquerors that parade
through his work: Lowell ransacked history and filled the pages
of his poems with their names.

Alexander extended philosophy
farther than Aristotle or the honest man,
and kept his foot on everything he touched—
                    ("Poor Alexander, poor Diogenes," *H* 40)

Throw Hannibal on the scales, how many pounds
does the First Captain come to?
                    ("Hannibal 2. The Life," *H* 42)

Am I your only lover who always died?
We were right to die instead of doing nothing,
fearfully backstepping in the dark night of lust.
                    ("Antony," *H* 45)

My namesake, Little Boots, Caligula,
tell me why I got your name at school—
                .   .   .
my namesake, not the last Caligula.
                    ("Caligula 2," *H* 48)

Robespierre could live with himself: "The republic
of Virtue without *la terreur* is a disaster.
                    ("Robespierre and Mozart as Stage," *SP* 171)

Charles had himself strapped to the saddle . . . bound to death,
his cavalry that scorned the earth it trod on.
                    ("Colonel Charles Russell Lowell 1835–64," *H* 88)

Custer, leaping with his wind-gold scalplock,
half a furlong or less from the Sioux front line,
and Sitting Bull, who sent our rough riders under—
both now dead drops in the decamping mass. . . .
                    ("1930's [My legs hinge]," *SP* 190)

                    I'm scared
of hitting this street, his street so far to our left
in gala anti-Stalinist 1950—
I wouldn't murder and be murdered for my soul,
like Stonewall Jackson sucking the soul of a lemon. . . .
                    ("F. O. Matthiessen 1902–50," *H* 134)

    The details Lowell chose in depicting these men, especially
the "tyrants," tell us what he thought they got out of their

position, the kind of freedom he imagined them to have. In "Stalin," Lowell says, "What raised him/ was an unusual lust to break the icon,/ joke cruelly, seriously, and be himself" (*SP* 179). Of DeGaulle he writes that he was "free/ to piss in any direction on your lawn" ("DeGaulle's Chienlit," *H* 190). These men created for themselves, through the exercise of their power, the opportunity to do what they wanted, when they wanted. Nobody could contradict them or check their desires. Their only barrier, in a world of boundaries, was mortality.

❧

Lowell failed to integrate the sonnets in *Notebook* as Berryman did *The Dream Songs* through the modulations of an off-center voice whose guffaws and asides and sadnesses are made possible by the narrators, Henry and Mr. Bones. Lowell tried instead to make something more like *The Cantos*, where the poet can bring the jumbledness of his own memory and the pressure of the instant to bear as stanchions. Pound at least is sufficiently obscure to us, and uncovers resonant names, brings the dead back to life because of what they stood for, not who they were. In this sense Lowell capitalizes on Pound's expansion of the limits of the medium° more than he mines them. "Malatesta," for Pound, is an emblem, a model ruler who supported the arts and who used his power discerningly; Stalin, Attila, and Hitler, for Lowell, are mere power figures, military men, conquerors who dominated by force.

It is difficult to puzzle out the reasons for Lowell's obsession with men of power. Does the same man who judged his own father so harshly think of Attila the Hun, Hitler, or Stalin as beyond morality? Or does his attitude reiterate history's?

What's he up to anyway? What's he trying to say? And does it cohere?

ATTILA, HITLER

Hitler had fingertips of apprehension,
"Who knows how long I'll live? Let us have war.
We *are* the barbarians, the world is near the end."
Attila mounted on raw meat and greens
galloped to massacre in his single fieldmouse suit,
he never left a house that wasn't burning,
could only sleep on horseback, sinking deep
in his rural dream. Would he have found himself
in this coarsest, cruelest, least magnanimous,
most systematic, most philosophical . . .
a nomad stay-at-home: *He who has, has;*
a barbarian wondering why the old world collapsed,
who also left his festering fume of refuse,
old tins, dead vermin, ashes, eggshells, youth?

(*SP* 163)

Lowell attempts to characterize the two most notorious "barbarians" who ever lived in fourteen lines and ends with a wry self-portrait. Hitler, like Napoleon, is *logical* and proceeds from thought to action. But Attila is comprehensible to Lowell precisely where Hitler is not. The poem is an attempt to put Hitler into historical perspective, and it centers around the conjecture that Hitler may have used Attila as his inspiration. The assertion underneath the question is that Hitler would be inconceivable without Attila.

Look at the differences between their relative fields of action. Hitler senses that when we're so close to apocalypse the time is right for barbarism to take root. And his motives stem directly from the self: "Who knows how long I'll live?" The best thing in the poem is the portrait of Attila, who is driven by primitive desires. He's methodical; a part of his horse, like a centaur, he always had to be on top even when asleep. He lives by the law of the jungle: if I take it I've got it. What does he dream about riding across the barren plain? Home.

Phrases like "single fieldmouse suit" and "he never left a house that wasn't burning" have the kinds of details that give Lowell's historical sonnets character, in both senses of the word. The ideas, in this poem, are less interesting than the details, and the second half is disappointing at the level of details, ideas, and language. It's as if Lowell had been defeated by the form. The poem could have been shorter or longer.

It is hard to posit another direction for him, but in these sonnets there is a feeling of anxiety and of his being cut off from his unconscious. Many of the sonnets have a quality of workmanship, of him doing a job, of getting down the words. You don't feel that he is *given* to write these sonnets in the way Berryman was given to write *The Dream Songs* or Pound *The Cantos.* Poetry becomes something he does day by day. The faults of Lowell's sonnets that don't work can be "summed up by the word *jerky*," a phrase he used to pinpoint the defects he saw in the poetry of Ralph Gustafson in an early review of his work. They fail because the material lacks internal connection, organic form. His choices are too often arbitary, as can be seen from the many revisions where he reversed the meaning of a line or phrase.

But when he's engaged he hurls us into a fully imagined scene wherein the language and the action feel inseparable. The sounds of the words mate with the landscape. He is free to work within his own system. He's no longer tied, to narrative, like Turner to the mast.

LONG SUMMERS

Months of it, and the inarticulate mist so thick
we turned invisible to one another
across the room; the floor, aslant, shot hulling
through thunderheads, gun-cotton dipped in pitch,

salmon, when lighted, as the early moon,
snuffed by the malodorous and frosted murk—
not now! Earth's solid and the sky is light,
yet even on the steadiest day, dead noon,
the sun stockstill like Joshua's in midfield,
I have to brace my hand against a wall
to keep myself from swaying—swaying wall,
straitjacket, hypodermic, helmeted
doctors, one crowd, white-smocked, in panic, hit,
stop, bury the runner on the cleated field.

(*SP* 191)

Even though the poem is in a section called *Nineteen Thirties*, I think that it begins much later and takes place in Maine where the fog lingers and fills the room. And if it doesn't actually last for months it feels like months. The *t* sounds slow the movement down. The tongue presses itself against the roof of the mouth.

Fog-soaked! Dominated by nature. If the first line weren't there we'd think we were in another psychological poem about estrangement. The "it" refers to the mood the weather brings on. "It" makes him desperate for connection; "inarticulate" suggests that circumstances beyond his control have taken over. The "I" and the "we" have grown apart and been separated inside the same space. It may be no more than severely warped soft wood that transforms the floor into an active, violent force to counteract the weary stasis of the first two and a half lines. Lowell conjures storms, battles, and seeks to find resemblances between the natural and the unnatural. He portrays the color of the room under lamplight, that is, when lights are on the fog in the room turns as salmon-colored as the rising moon. But this particular glow is perceptible only when "the early moon,/ snuffed by the malodorous and frosted murk—" is at its lowest level of visibility. The dash after "murk" means he can't continue to stretch these comparisons and remain articulate. He hangs himself on that dash: "malodorous and frosted murk" is too much. Even Hamlet's father can say "sulphurous and tormenting flames" because he's a dead father, a ghost, and parents and adolescents are allowed this sort of grand exaggeration anyway. But "not now!" When invention flags he has to face the day. "Not now" alerts us to a time shift. *Then* was during the long summers of borderline madness, but even now—when his rational light is bright—he has to steady himself by hanging on to the wall.

The lines that follow (7, 8, and 9) are back up to the standard set by the first three. There are limits to projection. The sun has burned through the mist and other terrors encroach. He sets the scene for the great battle, the final encounter that will settle everything, and he prepares us for it with these stately cadences: "Earth's solid and the sky is light,/ yet even on the steadiest day, dead noon,/ the sun stockstill like Joshua's in midfield."

The reference to Joshua, Moses' protégé and successor, alludes to the battle of Jericho that was to take place on a Friday, and is about the power of prayer. Since God would not allow fighting on the Sabbath, Joshua prayed that the sun would not set—to prolong the day for the purpose of winning the battle. Control of the day is a metaphor for the control of time. Who can control a moment of time? No man. But through prayer (and with God on his side) Joshua did: once.

Lowell's tone is prophetic. In *Lord Weary's Castle* his voice had the affect of prophecy. The style belied it. The biblical prophets were men who walked among men. They said disjointed things, they didn't recite speeches. They were wanderers and solitaries who were wont to participate in the human community only when they were convinced it was necessary. They used present instances to demonstrate deeper truths. In times of stress they heard voices, sensed what had been censored around them, went among men (direct encounters were the only way to communicate then), told what they had heard from urgent sources, and tried to agitate "the people" out of torpor and short-sightedness. The Biblical heroes like Moses and Joshua (to whom Lowell refers in "Long Summers") did many of the same things and were able to *act* as well.

But Lowell loses control—"I have to brace my hand against a wall/ to keep myself from swaying"—struggles to steady himself to no avail—"swaying wall"—remembers the worst: what these fits can lead to—"straitjacket, hypodermic, helmeted/ doctors, one crowd, white-smocked." And then heroically he manages to follow through with the scene out of the Biblical past he'd referred to before everything starts to sway against his will, and makes the necessary connection between the outlets for violence in the past, brutal but prompted by necessity, and our present forms of ritualized violence: "in panic, hit,/ stop, bury the runner on the cleated field." There the modern hero lies, surrounded by cheerleaders who bite their lower lips when the wounded athlete/victim is carried away on a stretcher.

Robert Lowell spent his life at that tragic intersection, dispelling, casting spells on "the Black Widow, death" ("Mr. Edwards and the Spider," *SP* 28). And

> The line must terminate.
> Yet my heart rises, I know I've gladdened a lifetime
> knotting, undoing a fishnet of tarred rope;
> the net will hang on the wall when the fish are eaten,
> nailed like illegible bronze on the futureless future.
>
> ("Fishnet," *SP* 227)

The fish are the life out of which he makes his art; the "fishnet of tarred rope" is his legacy.

CHAPTER 5

Inextinguishable Roots

One must not come to feel that he has a thousand threads
  in his hands,
He must somehow see the one thing;
This is the level of art
There are other levels
But there is no other level of art

—George Oppen

Part of the tragedy of Lowell's death at sixty is that he was on
his way to becoming a great poet of old age: mellow, reflective,
funny, and always—could he be else?—intense. The poems in
Day by Day are mainly meditations on past actions. Although
there are a few grim harbingers of death, the book is about living out the afterlife in this life.

> We asked to be obsessed with writing,
> and we were.
>
> Do you wake dazed like me,
> and find your lost glasses in a shoe?
>> ("For John Berryman"
>> [After reading his last *Dream Song*], *DBD* 27)
>
> Being old in good times is worse
> than being young in the worst.
>> ("In the Ward" [For Israel Citkovitz], *DBD* 38)

> I can see through the moonlit dark;
> on the grassy London square,
> black cows ruminate in uniform,
> lowing routinely like a chainsaw.
> My visitors are good beef, they too make
> one falsely feel the earth is solid,
>
> ("Visitors," *DBD* 110)

> Under New York's cellular façades
> clothed with vitreous indifference,
> I dwindle . . . dynamite no more.

> I ask for a natural death,
> no teeth on the ground,
> no blood about the place . . .
> It's not death I fear,
> but unspecified, unlimited pain.
>
> ("Death of a Critic," *DBD* 48)

All his life Lowell was trying to become comfortable with imperfection and in *Day by Day* he does. The book was an open door for him and it contains the most flexible verse he ever wrote. The fourteen-line girdle is gone. While retaining always the integrity of the line, he seemed to let his thoughts drift where they would, sometimes dredging, sometimes drifting, but following his Muse. Many of the poems directly confront the question of his art—but he gives himself the freedom here that he sought in *Life Studies* and then backed away from in successive books. Some of the key poems are "Ulysses and Circe," "Last Walk," "Since 1939," "Art of the Possible," "In the Ward," "Death of a Critic," "Domesday Book," "The Spell," "The Withdrawal," "Wellesley Free," "Grass Fires," "Turtle," "Visitors," "Shifting Colors," and "Unwanted."

As with *Life Studies* and *History*, the first poem in *Day by Day*, "Ulysses and Circe," contains a line that could define Lowell's stance in the book: "Risk was his métier" (*DBD* 8). Gifted with an associative mind, he had previously shackled himself

with fixed subject matter and forms. The formal devices used in
these late poems are exaggerated versions of his earlier style. He
uses more syntactical ambiguity in these poems; more unfin-
ished thoughts, unusual line breaks, and enforced pauses between statements.

> the houses still burn
> in the golden lowtide steam of Turner.
> Only when we start to go,
> do we notice the outrageous phallic flare
> of the splash flowers that fascinated children.
>
> The reign of the kingfisher was short.
>
> ("Domesday Book," *DBD* 56)

"Domesday Book" is a gallant (rather than a chivalrous) poem
and the language in it is unusually rich for late Lowell. In this
passage he is saying that it's too painful to perceive the ubiquitous sexuality of "splash flowers," leaving the reader to fill in the
adjectives this time—colorful, wet, startling, dazzling, agi-
tated—and implying that we spend our lives holding our ears
lashed to the mast like Ulysses confronted with the Sirens. Image the third line as

> Only   when   we   start   to   go

and we can see why the phrase is so charged—direct and suggestive. Here, words are particles that take hold of the air and never
let go. "Outrageous phallic flare/ of the splash flowers" stands
for excess and exhaustion, desire and death, the longing to return to childhood undercut by the rasp of the aside which re-
fuses this poet the balm of nostalgia. Intensity precludes longev-
ity. The lumbering turtle, not the darting kingfisher, lives a long
time. But the real risk, as Lowell perceived it, was to distin-
guish, for the poem, memory from imagination, fact from truth.
Blake, for one, made a clear distinction between the two. Did

Lowell? Lowell worried that he had become too reliant on "the threadbare art of [his] eye," and paralyzed by the facts he recorded:

> But nature is sundrunk with sex—
> how could a man fail to notice, man
> the one pornographer among the animals?
> I seek leave unimpassioned by my body,
> I am too weak to strain to remember, or give
> recollection the eye of a microscope. I see
> horse and meadow, duck and pond,
> universal consolatory
> description without significance,
> transcribed verbatim by my eye.
>
> ("Shifting Colors," *DBD* 119–20)

In "Jean Stafford, a Letter" (*DBD* 29), Lowell reveals an aspect of his first wife's character through the way she pronounced the name of the German novelist—

> *Towmahss Mahnn:* that's how you said it . . .
> "That's how Mann must say it," I thought.

The correct pronunciation of foreign names signifies different things in different contexts. It can be seen as a sign of intellectual and cultural sophistication, traits that Lowell found attractive in women. But, read in conjunction with the ensuing lines, it can also be seen as a sign of affectation.

> I can go on imagining you
> in your Heidelberry braids and Bavarian
> peasant aprons you wore three or four years
> after your master's at twenty-one.

This description is less compelling than the initial memory in the first two lines, but it does show, without showing, how he sees her clinging to her student years, her specialness and precocity. And given his earlier rendition of their relationship in

"The Old Flame," "quivering and fierce . . . simmering like wasps/ in our tent of books!" (*SP* 102), I can imagine him pointing out to her the very details in Mann's *Tonio Kröger*, which he later appropriated for "The Exile's Return," such as "Not ice, not snow," showing how the fiction writer can show without showing.

And yet the "facts" in these final poems are never recorded—they are blessedly smudged by imagination. That's the sign of a powerful imagination—the ability to transform memory in the process of recollection—to give it form: to sing. In "The Withdrawal" (*DBD* 73), when Lowell looks back, he sees "a collapsing/ accordion of my receding houses," a whole life—

> and myself receding
> to a boy of twenty-five or thirty,
> too shopworn for less, too impressionable for more—
> blackmaned, illmade
> in a washed blue workshirt and coalblack trousers

Lowell continues to hit the nerve of what we can never know about ourselves: the selves he remembers are always imagined, decisively seen, perceived, rendered, but not fixed or unidimensional. The movement forward in time and the movement backward are one and the same. The body moves forward in space, the imagination backward in time, and, in the gap between the remembered scene and the feeling, Lowell leaves white space replete with significance and without pretension.

> moving from house to house,
> still seeking a boy's license
> to see the countryside without arrival.
>
> Hell?

Hell—it rhymes with "arrival." And yet to see the countryside/hell without being there is disconcerting. The cost of Lowell's self-estrangement is that the body and mind have never been one, but is there anyone who does not suffer from this malady? Only one who, like the narrator of Beckett's *How It Is*, can exist wholly in the present tense, like the ocean, someone who just *is;* to be in that condition of being one must put aside all worldliness, all remorse.

In *Day by Day* Lowell begins to make use of depression and aging much in the same way Beckett made use of impotence and despair. Beckett's cosmic anguish is more interesting than Lowell's personal depression and yet Lowell appeals to our common humanity. He engages us with his unanswered, unanswerable questions—alternating currents of pain and doubt.

> I was surer, wasn't I, once . . .
> and had flashes when I first found
> a humor for myself in images,
> farfetched misalliance
> that made evasion a revelation?
>
> ("Unwanted," *DBD* 121)

I think that the key to the change in the style and tone of *Day by Day* can be found in his translation of Aeschylus' Orestean trilogy, where the Chorus states: "A man must kill now to live" (*OA* 63). And Orestes, like Colonel Robert Gould Shaw, continues in Lowellian fashion: "By the immortals, by my hands! . . . I want/ to take her life and die" (*OA* 67). Lowell turned to the Greeks for fierceness and to help him refashion his vision to one closer to prepsychoanalytic man. In this spirit Lowell has Orestes say: "Nothing can atone for one act of murder." The harshness of this attitude is closest to Lowell's own. As Richard Pevear has observed in another context, "Perhaps, as the Greeks thought, time does not alter the condition of being human." In spite of the determinedly Oedipal constructions, *Day by Day*, like *Life Studies*, is antipsychotherapeutic. Throughout both books, Lowell used the "talking cure"—free association, the stock device of Freudian and most post-Freudian psychotherapy—to unearth memories, as a means toward an artistic end rather than a therapeutic one.

In the first poem in *Day by Day*, "Ulysses and Circe," Lowell moves from the frantic, everyday world of the previous books into the mythic "surge." As in his early poems, the story has a built-in conflict which gives Lowell's fierce combustible emotion a structure in which to rise and fall, painfully, abruptly. Lowell has been islanded in England just as Ulysses was on Circe's isle. But where Ulysses is sent off to consult Tiresias in Hades, though no man before him had ever sailed to the land of the dead, Lowell, in the course of the book, goes to confront his own impinging death.

> Age is the bilge
> we cannot shake from the mop.

(V, *DBD* 7)

Throughout "Ulysses and Circe," Lowell stays with the pivotal conflict, casting himself as Ulysses with, possibly, his third wife as Circe and his second wife as the offstage Penelope. As before, the real enemies are time and death, but here the conflicts are imaged through nature, as when

> The sun rises,
> a red bonfire,
> weakly rattling in the lower branches—
> that eats like a locust and leaves the tree entire.

(II, *DBD* 3)

Lowell's old redness, which has appeared in so many forms and guises, is now reflective of age, "weakly rattling," although his imagination, in the deft transposition of a visual image into sound, is in no way diminished. Lowell renders this dawn in language exactly as our senses perceive it. He turns the sound of "rattling" into sight, and respects the reader, whom he assumes will have seen branches rattling in the wind and bonfires crackling, and leaves himself free to shift the emphasis, opening his ears and ours to a fresh idea about how language works in relation to the senses.

When I first read *Day by Day*, I found it unbearably painful and had to put it down. Three years passed before I could read it again. "Unwanted," coming late in the book, is probably the most important single poem as well as the grimmest.

> Too late, all shops closed—
> I alone here tonight on *Antabuse*,
> surrounded only by iced white wine and beer,
> like a sailor dying of thirst on the Atlantic—
> one sip of alcohol might be death,
> death for joy.
>
> (*DBD* 121)

This is the ultimate hell for Lowell. *Antabuse*, with its connotations of opposition and punishment, is a long way from *Miltown*. And if the poem does liven up in spurts, the beginning and the end are as bleak as hell. We know how much desperation a foreigner feels (I assume he wrote this in England) to discover (away from home, traveling, or even at home) that it's "Too late, all shops closed." The poet is stuck with himself at a time when he needs to be distracted or be among others. "Too late" also reflects his attitude toward his life as a whole, echoing "Never to have lived is best" from "Between the Porch and the Altar"— though Lowell held out hope that his life would change, that he would be lifted out of the mire. Later in the poem he recalls:

> That year Carl Jung said to mother in Zurich,
> "If your son is as you have described him,
> he is an incurable schizophrenic."

I don't think "an incurable schizophrenic" could rhyme "Zurich" and "schizophrenic," but Lowell lived in terror of the mania and depression that so often came to overtake him. As for the final truth about the validity of his mother's perception of him: "One thing is certain—compared with my wives,/ mother was stupid." Even though he adds a qualifying "Was she?" as he scrutinizes her through the eyes of others ("Some would not have judged so—/ among them, her alcoholic patients,/ those raconteurish, old Boston young men"). He had come to see her in this new light.

The problem isn't just what Lowell calls "misalliance" ("Epilogue," *DBD* 127). Listen:

> We feel the machine slipping from our hands,
> as if someone else were steering;
> if we see a light at the end of the tunnel,
> it's the light of an oncoming train.
>
> ("Since 1939," *DBD* 31)

This is clearly a prefiguration of his own death, but maybe "someone else" has always been steering and Lowell hasn't known or wouldn't acknowledge it. Coming at the end of a poem which begins with a memory of leafing "through the revolutionary thirties'/ *Poems* of Auden," whom he sees "historical now as Munich," "the machine" is THE MACHINE, history as mechanism, with those two "Scythers, time and death," as the cogs and prime movers.

Lowell refused to accept death as inevitable. Well—it is. And it's not just a matter of complexity: he's unclear because he can't reconcile life and time and as a result one meaning often cancels out another. "Unwanted" continues:

> Mother,
> I must not blame you for carrying me in you
>
> . . .
>
> for yearning seaward, far from any home, and saying,
> "I wish I were dead, I wish I were dead."
> Unforgivable for a mother to tell her child—
>
> ("Unwanted," *DBD* 123)

The last stanza implicates us all:

> Is the one unpardonable sin
> our fear of not being wanted?
> For this, will mother go on cleaning house
> for eternity, and making it unlivable?
> Is getting well ever an art,
> or art a way to get well?

These are the kinds of questions people ask themselves, wrestle with alone, and that also come up in conversation. But the precision and decisiveness of Lowell's phrasing and his placement of the questions in the poem put them into the realm of art even without the searing wit of "making it unlivable." We're drawn to him because we want to take part in the dialogue. Even the manner in which he writes down these unanswered questions engages us. He courts conclusions, and swerves away from resolution, pressing against the finality of absolutes.

As he sees himself growing older among the young, Lowell consistently refers to late middle age as old age. His moods vacillate, self-pity alternates with self-deprecating humor.

> The best machine can be wrecked
>
> at 56.
> I balance on my imbalance,

and count the black and white steps
to my single room.

      .   .   .

I have fallen from heaven.
In my overnight room,
3 French windows to the right,
and 3 to the left
cast bright oblique reflections
unnerving with their sparkle.

                    ("Wellesley Free" [A reading], *DBD* 76)

In this poem Lowell no longer has expectations with regard to the
coming encounter, in this case a poetry reading, but spends his
time anxiously worrying whether he will make it through the
ordeal without losing face. He tries not to worry, not to feel
absurd, tries to survive the night and in the process finds "use"
for his "sense of humor." Helen Vendler was right to call Lowell's mood in *Day by Day* Chekhovian. It is hard to imagine the
author of any of his previous books, with the possible exception
of *The Dolphin*, writing these lines with their hard, wry, un-
flinching ironic humor. He allows himself one classically fine
line, "cast bright oblique reflections," before dousing its sparkle
with the cold fact of his querulous emotional state.

But there is something to be said for the rejection of wisdom.

A lemon-squeezer night—

I cannot sleep solo,
I loathe age with terror,
and will be that . . .
eat the courage of my selfishness
unredeemed by the student's
questionmark potential . . .

70° outside,
and almost December.

In a way, to lose that "questionmark potential" is to lose everything, no matter how much he may have gained, because it leaves nothing to look forward to and the future becomes a closed door. "Unredeemed" is an important word choice for this once Catholic poet. What interests me is the shift from regret into a kind of wonder at the uncertainty of life reflected in the unseasonably warm early winter weather. Isn't that his real redemption as a man and a poet, the part of him that can and will submit to change and go through, rather than around, the despair and anxiety that precede growth and acceptance? Isn't that a valid form of hope or a genuine expression of it? In "Visitors" these lines emerge while he's being wheedled "into a stretcher."

> I lie secured there, but for my skipping mind.
> They keep bustling.
> "Where you are going, Professor,
> you won't need your Dante."

("Visitors," *DBD* 111)

When in reality he will need it more than ever.

※※※

In these late poems the once never to be "cowed" Robert Lowell is never free from anxiety in the present tense. Self-awareness is no help to a man in this state of being and that perception constitutes one of Lowell's major contributions to what R. P. Blackmur called the stock of available reality.

In *Notebook* he was often pricked by the intrusion of a memory because it took him out of the present and then dropped him back down in an unfamiliar and therefore painful ambiance—the present, replacing the time he left behind. In *Day by Day* he is at ease with the to and fro sway of memory, reflection; he is, in essence, keenly interested, alert. Look at "Grass Fires."

> In the realistic memory
> the memorable must be foregone;
> it never matters,
> except in front of our eyes.
>
> ("Grass Fires," *DBD* 85)

Or: out of sight out of mind. Horror to behold such a thought! The poem continues:

> We cannot recast the faulty drama,
> play the child,
> unable to align
> his toppling, elephantine script,
> the hieroglyphic letters
> he sent home.

This is done with Prosperian ease and the key lies in his attitude toward his life: the drama is over. Even the harmony he conceives is connected to his decision to accept the ravages of time in relation to his body. In late middle age he is no longer tormented by anticipation, "hand on glass/ and heart in mouth . . . too boiled and shy/ and poker-faced to make a pass" ("Man and Wife," *SP* 93). The pain in *Day by Day* doesn't sting. There are no answers but the questions remain, and the feelings remain, inside the images:

> I hold big kitchen matches to flaps of frozen grass
> to smoke a rabbit from its hole—
> then the wind bites them, then they catch,
> the grass catches, fire everywhere,
> everywhere
> inextinguishable roots,
> the tree grandfather planted for his shade,
> combusting, towering
> over the house he anachronized with stone.
>
> ("Grass Fires," *DBD* 85)

The rhythm is natural and relaxed. We no longer feel Lowell to be working so hard to achieve an effect and the result is majestic. Prior to *Day by Day* Lowell would never have left the second "everywhere" there to catch his crucial second thoughts, since the main point of his commitment to the particular was his belief that if you touched the point of pain it spread everywhere and that everyone was graced and afflicted with "inextinguishable roots," something most people would like to forget—not their origins but that nothing can be undone. Let me put it another way. Lowell remembered the essential; he didn't always know what it meant but he would uncover something in the process of remembering that more programmatic minds weed out before they get to the unknowable sludge, the "dark downward and vegetating kingdom" ("For the Union Dead," *SP* 135), wherein the mystery resides.

Despite his immersion in the quotidian, in this book Lowell is not writing for himself as in a journal, jotting down whatever comes into his head and then sifting through it for good lines. He simultaneously addresses others and himself, his inner self, his deep invisible "I." His candor is endearing, but lends no real transparency. Many of the poems remain opaque and mysterious, prismatic, riddled with possibilities of meaning which he doesn't attempt to clarify.

Even at the end of the book Lowell still fears that he hasn't submitted the data to the transforming power of the imagination, and to this fear there is no absolute or final answer. He worries that his work is too close to life and, consequently, not art: "everything I write/ . . . seems a snapshot,/ . . . paralyzed by fact." But what Lowell calls memory could be called imagination.

> Yet why not say what happened?

The criticism that he levels against himself in "Epilogue" pertains more to his past than his present work, faults he had overcome after the relentlessly willed decade of fourteen-liners and the "relevent" poetry of the late sixties. I think that Lowell was in a transitional phase, in the process of becoming a meditative poet, unfamiliar with his own emerging self and poetic voice, unable to evaluate its quality, and that he had already achieved "the grace of accuracy" he aspired to when he seized Vermeer's eternal moment in these lines, as "the sun's *illumination*"—not the sun—is "stealing like the tide across a map/ to his girl solid with yearning." Lowell died after having once again opened up some new terrain for poetry and the poetic imagination to explore.

EPILOGUE
Those blessèd structures, plot and rhyme—
why are they no help to me now
I want to make
something imagined, not recalled?
I hear the noise of my own voice:
The painter's vision is not a lens,
it trembles to caress the light.
But sometimes everything I write
with the threadbare art of my eye
seems a snapshot,
lurid, rapid, garish, grouped,
heightened from life,
yet paralyzed by fact.
All's misalliance.
Yet why not say what happened?
Pray for the grace of accuracy
Vermeer gave to the sun's illumination
stealing like the tide across a map
to his girl solid with yearning.

We are poor passing facts,
warned by that to give
each figure in the photograph
his living name.

(*DBD* 127)

Notes

INTRODUCTION

1. Jacques Lacan, *Écrits: A Selection*, trans. Alan Sheridan (New York: Norton, 1977), p. 167.

2. Charles Baudelaire, "Le Cygne," available in Elaine Marks, ed., *French Poetry from Baudelaire to the Present* (New York: Dell, 1962), p. 58 (I, line 22).

3. Ibid., p. 59 (II, lines 4–7).

4. James Atlas, *Delmore Schwartz: The Life of an American Poet* (New York: Farrar, Straus and Giroux, 1977), p. 264.

CHAPTER 1. THE FALLEN CHRISTIAN

1. Robert Lowell, "Thomas, Bishop, and Williams," *Sewanee Review*, 55 (1947), p. 495.

2. Robert Hass, "One Body: Some Notes on Form," *Antaeus*, no. 30/31 (Spring 1978), p. 338.

3. Dante, *The Divine Comedy*, trans. Charles S. Singleton (Bollingen Paperback; Princeton: Princeton University Press, 1980), pp. 24–25.

4. Robert Lowell, transcribed from *Robert Lowell: A Reading* (Caedmon Records).

5. Thomas Mann, "Tonio Kröger," *Death in Venice and Seven Other Stories*, trans. H. T. Lowe-Porter (New York: Vintage, 1954), p. 78.

6. Ibid., p. 111.

7. Ibid., p. 76.

8. D. C. Gunby, *John Webster: Three Plays* (Harmondsworth, Middlesex, England: Penguin Books, 1972), pp. 15–16.

9. Ovid, *Metamorphoses*, trans. Arthur Golding as it appears in "The Source of *The Tempest*," in Robert Langbaum, ed., *The Tempest* (New York: Signet Classics, 1964), p. 139.

10. Samuel Taylor Coleridge, *The Lectures of 1811–1812, Lecture IX*, reprinted in *The Tempest*, p. 146.

11. E. A. Watkins, *Catholic Art and Culture* (London: Hollis and Carter, 1947), p. 177.

12. T. S. Eliot, "Little Gidding" from *Four Quartets*, in *The Complete Poems and Plays: 1909–1950* (New York: Harcourt, Brace, 1952), pp. 144–45 (V, lines 23–24).

13. Robert Lowell, review of "Four Quartets," *Sewanee Review*, 51 (1943), pp. 432 and 434.

14. T. S. Eliot, *Ash Wednesday*, in *The Complete Poems and Plays: 1909–1950*, pp. 60–61, I, line 21.

15. Ibid., I, lines 24–25.

16. Ibid., I, line 38.

17. Ibid., II, lines 8–11.

18. Robert Lowell, "After Enjoying Six or Seven Essays on Me," *Salmagundi*, no. 37 (Spring 1977), p. 114.

19. Ian Hamilton, "Conversation with Robert Lowell," *Modern Occasions*, 2 (Winter 1972), p. 36.

20. Leon Edel, *Henry James, The Conquest of London: 1870–1881* (New York: Avon, 1978), p. 78.

21. W. H. Auden and Norman Holmes Pearson, eds., *Elizabethan and Jacobean Poets: Marlowe to Marvell*, vol. 2 (New York: Viking, 1950), p. 18. The editors retained the old spelling and punctuation.

22. Louise Bogan, *A Poet's Alphabet*, ed. Robert Phelps and Ruth Limmer (New York: McGraw-Hill, 1970), p. 286.

23. William Carlos Willams, "The Descent," *Pictures from Brueghel: Collected Poems 1950–1962* (New York: New Directions, 1967).

CHAPTER 2. AN INTERRUPTED LIFE

1. William Gass, *Fiction and the Figures of Life* (New York: Vintage, 1971), p. 173.

2. Leo Tolstoy, *War and Peace*, trans. Ann Dunnigan (New York: Signet, 1968), p. 150.

3. Irvin Ehrenpreis, "The Age of Lowell," from *Stratford upon Avon* 7 (eds. John Russell Brown and Bernard Harris). Reprinted in Michael London and Robert Boyers, eds. *Robert Lowell: A Portrait of the Artist in His Time* (New York: David Lewis, 1970), p. 155.

4. Gary Snyder, *Six Sections from Mountains and Rivers Without End, Plus One*, rev. ed. (San Francisco: Four Seasons Foundation, 1970).

5. Gary Snyder, *Riprap & Cold Mountain Poems* (San Francisco: Grey Fox, 1965).

6. Baudelaire, "Le Voyage," in Marks, ed., *French Poetry*, p. 63 (I, lines 1–4).

7. Roland Barthes, *Roland Barthes*, trans. Richard Howard (New York: Hill and Wang, 1977), p. 51.

8. Helen Vendler, "Lowell in the Classroom," *The Harvard Advocate: Commemorative to Robert Lowell*, 113 (November 1979), p. 24.

9. Robert Lowell, "Visiting the Tates," *Sewanee Review*, 67 (1959), p. 557.

10. Octavio Paz, *The Bow and the Lyre* (Austin: University of Texas Press, 1973), p. 20.

11. Robert Lowell, "Thomas, Bishop, and Williams," *Sewanee Review*, 55 (1947), p. 498.

12. John Berryman, "Despondency and Madness: on Lowell's 'Skunk Hour,' " *The Freedom of the Poet* (New York: Farrar, Straus and Giroux, 1976), p. 319.

13. Elizabeth Bishop, "The Armadillo," *The Complete Poems* (New York: Farrar, Straus and Giroux, 1969).

14. Robert Lowell, "Epics," *The New York Review of Books*, 27, no. 2 (February 21, 1980), p. 3.

15. Stanley Kunitz, "Poet: A Conversation with Robert Lowell," in *A Kind of Order, A Kind of Folly* (Boston: Atlantic, Little, Brown, 1975), p. 154.

CHAPTER 3. THE DITCH IS NEARER

1. Jacques Lacan, *Écrits: A Selection*, trans. Alan Sheridan (New York: Norton, 1977), p. xi.

2. Stanley Kunitz, "Poet: A Conversation with Robert Lowell," *A Kind of Order, A Kind of Folly* (Boston: Atlantic, Little, Brown, 1975), pp. 154–55.

3. Robert Bly, "Robert Lowell's *For the Union Dead*," *Sixties*, no. 8 (1966), reprinted in Michael London and Robert Boyers, eds., *Robert Lowell: A Portrait of the Artist in His Time* (New York: David Lewis, 1970), pp. 72–73.

4. Thomas Hess, *Willem de Kooning* (New York: Museum of Modern Art, 1968), p. 45.

5. Malcolm Lowry, *Selected Letters of Malcolm Lowry*, ed. Harvey Breit and Margerie Bonner Lowry (Philadelphia and New York: J. B. Lippencott, 1965), p. 71.

6. William Blake, "Auguries of Innocence," available in *The Portable Blake* (New York: Viking, 1946), p. 150.

7. Blake, "London," *The Portable Blake*, p. 112.

8. Geoffrey H. Hartman, "The Eye of the Storm" (review of *For the Union Dead*), in *Partisan Review* 32 (Spring 1965), reprinted in London and Boyers, pp. 61–62.

9. Charles Baudelaire, "Anywhere Out of the World," in Elaine Marks, ed., *French Poetry* , p. 84.

10. Jacob Bronowski, *The Ascent of Man* (Boston: Little, Brown, 1974), pp. 115–16.

CHAPTER 4. WORDS MEAT-HOOKED FROM THE LIVING STEER

1. Stanley Kunitz, "Poet: A Conversation with Robert Lowell," in *A Kind of Order, A Kind of Folly*, p. 157.

2. Robert Lowell, "77 Dream Songs, John Berryman," *The New York Review of Books* 2, no. 8 (May 28, 1964), p. 3.

3. Ian Hamilton, "Conversation with Robert Lowell," *Modern Occasions*, 2 (Winter 1972), p. 31.

4. Elizabeth Bishop, "At the Fishhouses," *The Complete Poems* (New York: Farrar, Straus and Giroux, 1969).

5. Herakleitos, *Herakleitos and Diogenes*, trans. Guy Davenport (San Francisco: Grey Fox, 1979), no. 24.

6. Osip Mandelstam, "No. 78," *Mandelstam*, trans. Clarence Brown (Cambridge, Eng.: Cambridge University Press, 1973), p. 257.

7. Milan Kundera, *The Book of Laughter and Forgetting*, trans. Michael H. Heim (New York: Penguin, 1980), pp. 7–8.

8. Che Guevara, "Vietnam Must Not Stand Alone," *New Left Review* (London), no. 43 (1967), quoted in John Berger's essay " 'Che' Guevara," in *The Look of Things* (New York: Viking, 1974), p. 45.

9. Ibid.

10. Seamus Heaney, *Preoccupations* (New York: Farrar, Straus and Giroux, 1980), p. 223.

11. Wallace Stevens, "The Death of a Soldier," available in Stevens' *The Palm at the End of the Mind*, ed. Holly Stevens (New York: Vintage, 1972), p. 35 (line 7).

12. Wallace Stevens, "Esthétique du Mal," in *The Palm*, p. 256 (VII, lines 1–4).

Selected Bibliography

I. BIBLIOGRAPHIES

Mazzaro, Jerome. "A Checklist of Materials on Robert Lowell: 1939–1968." In Michael London and Robert Boyers, eds., *Robert Lowell: A Portrait of the Artist in His Time*. New York: David Lewis, 1970.

II. COLLECTIONS OF ESSAYS

Bedford, William, ed. *Agenda*, 18, no. 3 (Autumn 1980).

Boyers, Robert, ed. *Salmagundi*, no. 37 (Spring 1977). Special issue devoted to Lowell, including Robert Hass's fine essay "Lowell's *Graveyard*."

London, Michael, and Robert Boyers, eds. *Robert Lowell: A Portrait of the Artist in His Time*. New York: David Lewis, 1970. (Includes many essays and reviews, both positive and negative, by Lowell's contemporaries.)

Vendler, Helen. *Part of Nature, Part of Us: Modern American Poets*. Cambridge: Harvard University Press, 1980. (Includes essays on Lowell's later work.)

III. BOOKS ON LOWELL

Axelrod, Steven Gould. *Robert Lowell: Life and Art*. Princeton: Princeton University Press, 1978.

Cosgrave, Patrick. *The Public Poetry of Robert Lowell*. New York: Taplinger, 1972.

Hamilton, Ian. *Robert Lowell: A Biography*. New York: Random House, 1982.

Mazzaro, Jerome. *The Poetic Themes of Robert Lowell*. Ann Arbor: University of Michigan Press, 1965.

Perloff, Marjorie. *The Poetic Art of Robert Lowell*. Ithaca: Cornell University Press, 1973.

Staples, Hugh. *Robert Lowell: The First Twenty Years*. New York: Farrar, Straus & Cudahy, 1962.

Williamson, Alan. *Pity the Monsters*. New Haven: Yale University Press, 1974.

Yenser, Stephen. *Circle to Circle*. Berkeley and Los Angeles: University of California Press, 1975.

Index